A HISTORY OF
MULTICULTURAL AMERICA

Minorities
Today

William Loren Katz

RSVP
**RAINTREE
STECK-VAUGHN**
P U B L I S H E R S
The Steck-Vaughn Company

Austin, Texas

For Laurie

Cover and interior design: Joyce Spicer
Electronic production: Scott Melcer
Photo editor: Margie Foster
Photo research: Diane Hamilton

Library of Congress Cataloging-in-Publication Data

Katz, William Loren.
    Minorities today / by William Loren Katz.
       p.   cm. — (A History of multicultural America)
    Includes bibliographical references and index.
    Summary: Discusses the role of minorities and women in American history and society in this century's last decade, focusing on the experiences of Hispanic Americans, new European immigrants, Asian Americans, Native Americans, and others.
    ISBN 0-8114-6281-1   —   ISBN 0-8114-2918-0 (softcover)
    1. Minorities — United States — Juvenile literature.   2. United States — Ethnic relations — Juvenile literature.   3. United States — Race relations — Juvenile literature. [1. Minorities — History — 20th century.   2. Civil rights movements — History — 20th century.   3. Race relations. 4. United States — History — 1969-] I. Title.   II. Series: Katz, William Loren. History of multicultural America.
E184.A1K315   1993
305.8'00973—dc20   92-47438
                                                           CIP
                                                           AC

Printed and bound in the United States of America

1 2 3 4 5 6 7 8 9 0 LB 98 97 96 95 94 93

Acknowledgments

All prints from the collection of the author, William L. Katz, with the following exceptions: p. 7 © Bob Daemmrich/Stock Boston; p. 9 © Michael Dwyer/Stock Boston; p. 10 © Mary Kate Denny/PhotoEdit; p. 11 © Jerry Berndt/Stock Boston; p. 14 © 1992 The New York Times Company; pp. 15, 23, 41t, 42, 44 (both), 49b, 50, 53, 60, 63, 73, 76, 89, 93 Wide World; p. 18 © Carol Halebian/Gamma Liaison; p. 22, 48, 49t, 83, 84, 85 UPI/Bettmann; p. 24 © Richard Sobol/Stock Boston; p. 27 © Addison Geary/Stock Boston; p. 29 © Robert Brenner/PhotoEdit; p. 31© PJM/Stock Boston; p. 32 © Tony Freeman/PhotoEdit; p. 33 © Tony Freeman/PhotoEdit; p. 41b © JR Holland/Stock Boston; pp. 47, 59, 72, 77, 78, 87 Reuters/Bettmann; p. 52 © Brad Markel/Gamma Liaison; p. 65 © Will McIntyre/Photo Researchers; p. 70 © Carol Halebian/Gamma Liaison; p. 71 © Ken Ross/Gamma Liaison; p. 81 © Elizabeth Crews/Stock Boston; p. 82t © Richard Hutchings/PhotoEdit; p. 82b © David Young-Wolff/PhotoEdit; p. 86 © Carol Halebian/Gamma Liaison; p. 91 © Keith Jewell.

Cover: (inset) © Ron Sherman/Stock Boston; (map) © 1992 by The New York Times Company. Reprinted by permission.

TABLE OF CONTENTS

INTRODUCTION 4

1   PORTRAIT OF A PEOPLE 6

2   IMMIGRATION 10

3   HISPANIC AMERICA 14

4   AMERICANS FROM THE WEST INDIES 20

5   RUSSIAN AND IRISH IMMIGRANTS 24

6   ASIAN AMERICANS 27

7   ASIANS AND THE AMERICAN DREAM 33

8   NATIVE AMERICANS 39

9   AFRICAN AMERICANS 43

10 "RUN, JESSE, RUN" 51

11 ETHNIC SURVIVAL IN AMERICA 55

12 COMPETITIVE SPORTS IN AMERICA 59

13 JUSTICE IN AMERICA 61

14 AMERICAN EDUCATION 65

15 RACIAL CONFLICT AND COOPERATION 70

16 LOS ANGELES, 1992 75

17 AMERICAN WOMEN AT THE CROSSROADS 81

18 "THE YEAR OF THE WOMAN" 89

19 INTO THE 21ST CENTURY 92

FURTHER READING 94

INDEX 95

INTRODUCTION

The history of the United States is the story of people of many backgrounds. A few became wealthy through their knowledge of science, industry, or banking. But it was ordinary people who most shaped the progress of this country and created our national heritage.

The American experience, however, has often been recounted in history books as the saga of powerful men—presidents and senators, merchants and industrialists. Schoolchildren were taught that the wisdom and patriotism of an elite created democracy and prosperity.

A truthful history of the United States has to do more than celebrate the contributions of the few. Ordinary Americans fought the Revolution that set this country free, and ordinary workers built the nation's economy. The overwhelming majority of people held no office, made little money, and worked hard all their lives.

Some groups, women and minorities in particular, had to vault legal barriers and public hostility in order to make their contributions to the American dream, only to find that school courses taught little about their achievements. The valiant struggle of minorities and women to win dignity, equality, and justice often was omitted from history's account. Some believe this omission was accidental or careless, others insist it was purposeful.

Native Americans struggled valiantly to survive military and cultural assaults on their lives. But the public was told Native Americans were savages undeserving of any rights to their land or culture. African Americans battled to break the chains of slavery and to scale the walls of racial discrimination. But a century after slavery ended, some textbooks still pictured African Americans as content under slavery and bewildered by freedom. Arrivals from Asia, Mexico, and the West Indies faced legal restrictions and sometimes violence. But the public was told that they were undeserving of a welcome because they took "American jobs," and some were "treacherous aliens."

Whether single, married, or mothers, women were portrayed as dependent on men and accepting of a lowly status. The record of their sturdy labors, enduring strengths, and their arduous struggle to achieve equality rarely found its way into classrooms. The version of American history that reached the public carried many prejudices. It often preferred farmers over urban workers, middle classes over working classes, rich over poor. Women and minorities became invisible, ineffective, or voiceless.

This distorted legacy also failed to mention the campaigns waged by minorities and women to attain human rights. Such efforts did not reflect glory on white male rulers and their unwillingness to extend democracy and opportunity to others.

This kind of history was not a trustworthy tale. It locked out entire races and impeded racial understanding. Not only was it unreliable, but for most students it was dull and boring.

Our history has to be truthful and complete. Our struggle to overcome the barriers of nature and obstacles made by humans is an inspiring story. This series of books seeks to explore the heroic efforts of minorities and women to find their place in the American dream.

William Loren Katz

CHAPTER 1

PORTRAIT OF A PEOPLE

As of the last decade of the 20th century, the United States is the strongest power on the face of the earth. The giant Soviet Empire has disintegrated, and an era of international peace may be at hand. However, violence and discord based on ethnicity or religion continue to rage from Northern Ireland to Germany and from Bosnia to parts of the former Soviet Union. The term *ethnic cleansing* was the way one European army described its mission of destroying its enemy.

The United States of America and its many religions, races, and nationalities remains relatively peaceful. Some scholars argue that America's enduring strength has been built on its centuries as a multicultural democracy.

The 1990 United States Census pointed to profound changes in America. The population of the United States stood at about 249 million with 75 percent of the people listed as white. Nearly one in every four people claimed African, Asian, Hispanic, or Native American ancestry. In 1980 this figure was one in five Americans.

In 1990, there were 30 million African Americans, 22,400,000 Hispanic Americans, 7,300,000 Asian Americans, and 2 million Native Americans. Some 9,800,000 people classified themselves as "other race" — almost double the number who chose that category a decade earlier.

Between 1980 and 1990, the United States population increased by 9.8 percent. This growth was fastest among people of color. White Americans increased by 6 percent, African Americans by 13.2 percent, Native Americans by 37.9 percent, Asian Americans by 107 percent, and Hispanic Americans by 53 percent. Population diversity had grown so quickly that one authority hailed "the dawning of the first universal nation."

In population percentages, African Americans constituted 12 percent of the population and remained the largest racial minority. Hispanic Americans made up 9 percent of the population, Asian Americans 3 percent, and Native Americans .08 percent.

White Americans, 75 percent of the 1990 population, will enter the 21st century as a majority but will probably become a minority by its end. In 1990, statistics showed the number of white residents in 16 states declined, while 41 states showed a double-digit percentage growth for people of color.

Racial and ethnic changes are being accompanied by alterations in the geopolitical landscape of the United States. In the 1992 election, for the first time in history, there were more voters in suburbia than in cities.

Suburban growth and political power spell trouble now for inner cities. Inhabited by minorities and other poor people, ghetto neighborhoods seem less like the rest of the country and are being further isolated from political power. The future of American cities is increasingly decided by suburban voters and their representatives in state legislatures.

At the same time, both city and suburban communities have become less homogeneous and more diverse in ethnic composition. Neighborhoods in the United States are less likely to be segregated by race and more likely to be segregated by economic class.

Some states had become dramatically multicultural. Two-thirds of California's people were white in 1980, but the figure had fallen to 57 percent by 1990. Nearly 13 million of almost 30 million Californians were people of color. The state was home to 35 percent of the country's Hispanic American population and 39 percent of its Asian Americans.

Multicultural diversity is the hallmark of America in the last decade of the 20th century. In Austin, Texas, students and other community members speak out about the closing of their high school.

In 1990 racial minorities comprised 39 percent of the Texas population, 27 percent of Florida's population, and half of New Mexico's population. The figure for people of color in New York was 31 percent, a 20 percent increase in a decade. Minority growth in New Jersey and Connecticut was even higher. More Asian Americans lived in New York City than in Hawaii.

Beginning in 1990, the United States was hit by a business recession that cut across lines of race, religion, sex, age, and ethnicity. More than 14 percent of America's citizens fell below the federal government's poverty line. This figure did not include the homeless — who were usually not counted. By 1991, the real weekly wages of working people had declined 20 percent over the previous 15 years.

As poverty increased, wealth in America became more highly concentrated. One percent of the population owned 37 percent of the national wealth. The most affluent fifth of all households earned 46.5 percent of all household income, and the lowest fifth of households earned only 3.8 percent of the national income.

Poverty did not fall equally on each person or group. Though the poverty rate increased to 11.3 percent for whites in 1991, for people of color the statistics were disproportionately higher. African Americans had a poverty rate of 32.7 percent, Hispanic Americans 28.7 percent, and Asian Americans 13.3 percent.

Much had changed in a single generation. In 1973, 15 million whites, 7 million African Americans, and 2 million Hispanic Americans lived below the poverty line. In 1991, 24 million whites, 10 million African Americans, and 7 million Hispanic Americans were poor.

There were other signs of national economic weakness in 1990. About 35,700,000 Americans had no health insurance. Household purchasing power in two years had slumped by more than 5 percent for whites, African Americans, and Hispanic Americans and more than 8 percent for Asian Americans. Some 21.8 percent of the nation's children lived in poverty, more than any other age group. The elderly, those over 65, on the other hand, had a poverty rate of 12.4 percent.

Boston

Boston has long been called the "cradle of liberty" by many Americans because the American Revolution began there. In the early 19th century, tens of thousands of Irish immigrants arrived in Boston to make the port their home, and soon Irish American mayors ruled city hall. By the 1980s, Boston's Irish, Anglo-Saxon, and African American residents had been joined by newcomers from Vietnam, Haiti, Korea, the Philippines, the Dominican Republic, El Salvador, Puerto Rico, and Cambodia. Hispanic Americans constituted 10.8 percent of the population.

The census figures for 1990 showed that almost 40 percent of Boston's more than half a million people were members of minorities. The census indicated that by the year 2100, whites would be a minority. In the ten years between 1980 and 1990, the number of whites dropped about 8 percent to 62.8 percent of Boston's population, while the number of Asians more than doubled to 5.3 percent. Boston's African American population stood at 25.6 percent.

By 1990, several Irish American neighborhoods located in Boston had Vietnamese noodle shops and Spanish restaurants. East Boston, a largely Italian American neighborhood that was 98 percent white in 1980, had a population 17.6 percent Hispanic and 4 percent Asian in 1990.

Bennie Wiley, the president of Partnership, a Boston group that seeks to improve race relations, said, "Change is going to take people who are committed and focused for that to happen." In 1992, except for two African Americans, no people of color had ever won election to Boston's 13-member city council. "It is very much the old guard that's still in charge of the city," said Jaime Talero, the director of *Oficina Hispana*, a group representing the Hispanic Americans. "The Irish control politics, and the Yankees control the money."

Monica Castano, age 25, an immigrant from Colombia, moved to the city of Boston in 1990 where she enrolled in accounting and computer skills classes. She found a nonpaying one-day-a-week job there. When Ms. Castano asked her company for a paying job as an accounting clerk, she was told that her English was not good enough.

Boston's cultural organizations have begun to recognize the city's many minorities and to give them some consideration. The Museum of Fine Arts opened its first permanent gallery of African culture in the 1990s. ■

Boston residents of different ethnic backgrounds board buses near the Park Street Church, a famous historic landmark.

CHAPTER 2

IMMIGRATION

The United States is attracting immigrants at almost record levels as the 21st century approaches. More than 7 million people left their homelands for the United States in the 1980s. Not since the early 1900s had so many people arrived on American soil.

In 1989 alone, more than a million people set foot in the United States. Not since 1914 had so many come in a single year. People arrived from countries on five continents. Many came to live with their parents or family members who had migrated earlier. Mexicans constituted the largest group of immigrants, more than 405,000.

Under the Immigration Reform Law of 1986, 3.9 million illegal aliens were thought to be eligible for amnesty. Fifty-five percent of the eligible immigrants were from Mexico.

The number of arrivals who were refugees from oppression or war also increased sharply. More than half of all refugees came from the former Soviet Union, which faced wrenching political and economic changes. Other refugees poured in from strife-torn areas such as Laos, Vietnam, Cuba, Poland, Cambodia, Nicaragua, and Afghanistan. Ports of entry included New York, Miami, Los Angeles, Seattle, El Paso, Chicago, and San Diego.

In addition, more than a million immigrants living here in 1989 were granted permanent legal residence through the Immigration Reform Law of 1986. This act had been designed to grant legal status to Mexicans who might have entered illegally but had lived in the United States since 1982.

The newest arrivals spread out to every part of the nation, to cities, suburbs, and rural areas. Settlement patterns for groups varied. New York City became home for 115,759 Dominicans, or 61 percent of the total Dominican arrivals, 45 percent of the Jamaican immigrants, and 20 percent of the arrivals from China.

By 1990, New York City, which had received a million newcomers during the previous decade, had a foreign-born population of 28 percent. The sheer numbers of arrivals often overwhelmed immigration officials and city social services.

Most immigrants wanted to become citizens in the shortest possible time. In 1989 more than 230,000 foreigners were naturalized in the city. Marie De Targiani of the Catholic Migration Office in Brooklyn reported, "All the people are calling. All want to become instant citizens." In 1992, the New York *Daily News* reported, "Across the city, would-be citizens are crowding English classes and descending on immigration offices for application forms and interviews." The paper listed the 6 nations providing the city's largest number of naturalized citizens:

Dominican Republic	3,879
China	3,451
Jamaica	3,100
Guyana	2,994
Haiti	1,912
India	1,527

Reasons for seeking citizenship varied. Yun Zheng wanted to bring her aged parents from China. She failed the citizenship test the first time but had no intention of giving up.

> I have been studying so hard for this. Every night, I would just grab something to eat, and my 11-year-old daughter would help me study.

Edgar Noboa of Ecuador wanted to join the New York police force. He passed his test easily. Sylvio Maxi fled Haiti and wanted to take part in a democratic election. At 64, Pietro Mazzacappa from Italy had come to live near his two children. He passed his test and waited a month to take the oath of allegiance.

In 1991, 95,000 children of foreign birth entered the New York City school system. One in ten high school students in the city studied English as a Second Language. Teachers grappled with immense problems. Few teachers had the language skills necessary to deal with so many students who did not speak English. Many lacked an understanding of the vastly different cultures represented.

Some people who tried to assist new immigrants had themselves once fled their homelands. Lang Ngan

In U.S. schools immigrant children learn English as a Second Language.

left Saigon in 1974 with a blind father, a mother who weighed 78 pounds, and four sisters and brothers under the age of 13. She spoke enough English to be hired for a translating job and moved her family into an apartment in Queens, New York. In 1992, as a caseworker for the International Refugee Committee, Ngan devoted her life to helping other refugees. Those who come through Ngan's office in New York City were not from Asia but were mostly Ethiopians, Liberians, and Somalians. Yet Ngan found that, after all,

> They're like us — arranged marriages, eat a lot of rice, scared their children will go in the wrong direction, and don't speak English. The refugee experience is the same thing no matter where you come from — frustration, culture shock, sadness, upset stomach.

Ngan advises the arrivals on medical and emotional problems, and helps them get food stamps and social security cards. She also helps them adjust to buses, fast food, banks, and other aspects of American life.

To ease the way for newcomers, the American Museum of the Moving Image in Queens, New York, prepared a film program for Liberty High School in Manhattan, a school largely attended by immigrant children. Students were shown Charlie Chaplin's famous 26-minute silent film, *The Immigrant*, made in 1917. They watched as Chaplin, who himself had arrived from England a few years before 1917, dealt with a swaying ship, seasickness, and a bowl of soup that slid back and forth across a table as hungry immigrants stabbed at it with their spoons. Students watched Chaplin stare in wonder at the Statue of Liberty and saw him and other immigrants line up for a physical. They saw Chaplin finally reach the shore and eat a meal he couldn't pay for. Many students said they identified with the movie character who came expecting a life of ease and instead suddenly had to find money, a job, and a place to live.

Movies pictured other aspects of adjustment to America. *West Side Story*, a musical about Puerto Rican and white rivalry in New York City, was shown to the immigrants to help build their survival skills in a multicultural city. They also watched *Moscow on the Hudson* where comedian Robin Williams portrayed a Russian immigrant who is forced to take a variety of urban jobs.

After viewing the films, immigrant children discussed their experiences. Many said their high expectations did not match American reality. Odalise Santos from the Dominican Republic said,

> I...found everything different. They told me, "Oh, the life in the United States is so easy," and I didn't think so. They think you can get money when you want, jobs when you want. It's not like that.

Despite difficulties in adjusting to America, most immigrants arrived with high motivation and a strong desire to succeed. Their success rate, judged by statistics on self-employment, was often higher than that of other Americans. Self-employed means running your own business and is the aim of many Americans. Jamaican-born newcomers had a self-employment rate of 21 per thousand, higher than the 7.8 percent for black Americans and white Americans. Self-employment rates per thousand people are even higher among other ethnic groups: Chinese, 60.2; Cubans, 47.9; Greeks, 94.9; Japanese, 64.8; Lebanese, 106.6; Russians, 117.4; Syrians, 92.7; and Colombians, 30.1.

The Mixing Bowl

In 1991, the U.S. Immigration and Naturalization Service picked Elmhurst, Queens, with 114 different nationalities, as the most multicultural New York City neighborhood. "This is a mixing bowl of America," said Louie Antonio, a Greek immigrant whose thick cheese pizzas were very popular among East Indians.

Food often brings diverse cultures together. Elmhurst boasted Pakistani groceries, Colombian coffee shops, Thai seafood restaurants, Hong Kong noodle shops, and East Asian produce stores. One East Indian store displayed more than 100 varieties of pickles and 30 varieties of beans from India.

An Argentine bakery owned by a Korean, Siung Hong, was staffed by his son Paul and a young immigrant woman from Uruguay. It sells Argentine confections and sandwiches but is best known for its fine Jewish bagels and French croissants. Paul Hong said, "My father learned everything he knows at a Jewish bakery."

Reporter Dena Kleiman visited the New York City neighborhood. She concluded, "Here in Elmhurst the curious can find not only adventure and exotic fare but also concrete proof that the city's great melting pot happily bubbles on." ∎

CHAPTER 3

HISPANIC AMERICA

In 1990, 22,400,000 Hispanic Americans lived in the United States, an increase of 7.7 million people, or 53 percent more, in a decade. To the United States census, Hispanic Americans were people who speak Spanish or who were of Spanish, Portuguese, or Latin (Central or South) American descent. The census bureau estimated that the number of Hispanic Americans would reach 30 million by the year 2000. When they reach 40 million a decade after that, Hispanic and African Americans will each be 13 percent of the U.S. population.

Half of the enormous Hispanic American growth has been due to immigration, largely from Mexico. But the increase also resulted from a high birth rate and the federal government's legalization of new Hispanic American citizens. The census bureau also makes a special effort to count illegal aliens.

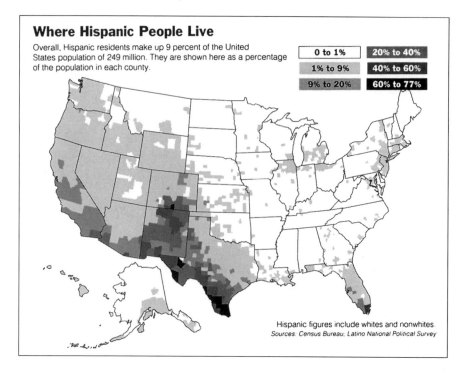

Where Hispanic People Live

Overall, Hispanic residents make up 9 percent of the United States population of 249 million. They are shown here as a percentage of the population in each county.

0 to 1%	20% to 40%
1% to 9%	40% to 60%
9% to 20%	60% to 77%

Hispanic figures include whites and nonwhites.
Sources: Census Bureau; Latino National Political Survey

In 1990, at least three-quarters of Hispanic Americans lived in the most populous states — Texas, California, New York, and Florida. Almost two-thirds live in 25 metropolitan areas. The largest number in any county, 3 million, lived in Los Angeles County. Dade County, Florida, had a Cuban American population of 950,000, and Cook County, Illinois, had almost 700,000. In both Rhode Island and Nevada, the number of Hispanic Americans rose by more than 130 percent, and in Virginia, New Hampshire, and Massachusetts the number of Hispanic Americans increased by more than 100 percent.

Hispanic American political power also had begun to grow with their increasing numbers. Mexican American women in Catholic parishes in San Antonio, Texas, mobilized a reform coalition called Communities Organized for Public Service (COPS) in 1973. After its first male leader, COPS chose five women presidents. In five years the coalition's reform ideas began to influence the San Antonio City Council. "It was a matter of tapping our networks," explained Beatrice Cortez, a former president of COPS.

A significant Mexican American victory came in 1983 with the election of Henry Cisneros as mayor of San Antonio. In 1984, Cisneros told the Democratic Party's national convention:

In 1983 Henry Cisneros was elected mayor of San Antonio, Texas.

> As a Hispanic American who has seen my city change for the better because of the Voting Rights Act, and who has seen children's futures brightened because of our national commitment to equal opportunity, I say sincerely to the black leaders and the black community of our nation, thank you, thank you for the sacrifices and the leadership that have opened up our country for the rest of us.
>
> Dr. King used to say that all America would be better because of what he was trying to do. Today, we know that countless thousands of women, Hispanics, Asian Americans, disabled persons, Native Americans, and working people...are better off because there was a civil rights movement, because the black community set the course for 20 years of change, and because Jesse Jackson ran for president in 1984.

Cisneros' election spurred new political efforts. By 1985, Hispanic Americans elected officials throughout the U.S. included

119 state executives and legislators and 1,316 county and city officials. In 1989, the number had risen to 133 state executives and legislators and 1,724 county and city officials. In 1993 Cisneros was named secretary of housing and human development by President Bill Clinton.

Hispanic America is becoming what Carlos Fuentes called "the fastest growing minority in the United States." In his 1992 book, *The Buried Mirror*, Fuentes defined Hispanic Americans:

> We are Indian, black, European, but above all mixed, mestizo. We are Iberian and Greek; Roman and Jewish; Arab, Gothic, and Gypsy. Spain and the New World are centers where multiple cultures meet — centers of incorporation, not of exclusion. When we exclude, we betray ourselves. When we include, we find ourselves.

Councilman Linares

Guillermo Linares, born in the coastal town of Cabrera in the Dominican Republic in 1951, left for the United States at 14 with his parents. The Linares family settled in the Bronx with other Dominican immigrants and took jobs in New York City's garment district.

Linares drove a gypsy cab, an unregistered taxi, for a living. At New York City College he studied to become a teacher and was president of the Dominican student society. After graduation, Linares became president of the District Six Board of Education, taught college courses, and took an interest in politics.

In 1991, Linares, 41, was elected to the New York City Council, the first Dominican American to win elective office in America. In July 1992, a policeman in Washington Heights killed Jose Garcia, a drug dealer. This triggered three nights of rioting. On the first night, Councilman Linares, holding two Dominican flags, led a march of protest. Unfortunately, the protest turned violent.

Linares set up a command post in Public School 28 where he worked to lessen community tensions. At a news conference with Mayor David Dinkins, Linares comforted the mother of the slain man. Then he stepped to the microphone and praised the police for handling matters calmly. "The best thing we have at this moment is that guy," said Luis Miranda, Jr., president of the Hispanic Federation of New York City. "He is a very calming person." A grand jury voted not to indict the policeman who shot Garcia, but the community remained calm. ■

Fuentes explained life within this growing community:

> Los Angeles is now the second-largest Spanish-speaking
> city in the world, after Mexico City, before Madrid and
> Barcelona. You can prosper in southern Florida even if
> you speak only Spanish, as the population is
> predominantly Cuban. San Antonio, integrated by
> Mexicans, has been a bilingual city for 150 years. By the
> middle of the coming century, almost half of the
> population of the United States will be Spanish-speaking.

Newly arrived Hispanic Americans have demonstrated an interest and skill in entrepreneurship. Their businesses earned more than $20 billion in 1990. Immigrant populations from Cuba, the Dominican Republic, and Nicaragua have been among the most enterprising of Americans. Yet, Fuentes points out, their traditional values remain strong:

> The family is regarded as the hearth, the sustaining
> warmth. It is almost a political party, the parliament of the
> social microcosm, and the security net in times of trouble.
> And when have times not been troubled?

The leading problem for Hispanic American arrivals in the United States has been learning English. Without knowing the English language, economic advancement remains a distant goal.

From California to New Mexico to New Jersey, Hispanic American immigrants often were exploited as agricultural laborers. In the Southwest, Cesar Chavez, founder and president of the United Farm Workers of America (UFWA), tried to unionize these workers for three decades. He repeatedly used boycotts and strikes to wrench concessions from employers. He said,

> Armed only with our unshakable commitment to a safe
> and just food supply, we've been struggling for 30 years
> on behalf of the poorest workers in the United States. Low
> wages, inhumane working conditions, exposure to toxic
> pesticides, and long hours of backbreaking labor by
> children are among the evils we've fought against.

To seek their American dream, some Mexican Americans have

Dennis Rivera, Labor Leader

One of America's most dynamic union figures in the 1990s was Dennis Rivera, born in Puerto Rico in 1951 to an Irish American father and a Puerto Rican mother. During the Vietnam War, Rivera received a student deferment and became an antiwar activist. He also joined the Puerto Rican Independence Party. Rivera became a labor organizer in San Juan when that job was so dangerous the young man had to carry a gun.

Rivera came to New York City in 1977. He found a job wheeling patients through hospital corridors at $270 a month and joined Local 1199 of the Drug, Hospital, and Health Care Employees Union.

In 1989, after a bitter union election campaign, Rivera was elected president of Local 1199. It was the largest health care union in the country, and its members included home care workers, registered nurses, pharmacists, some doctors, and service and maintenance workers.

Working as an official for the New York Democratic State Committee, Dennis Rivera helped elect David Dinkins mayor of New York City. Congressman Bill Richardson of New Mexico, head of the Hispanic Political Action Committee, said, "Dennis may not be an elected official, but he controls about nine million votes."

Rivera is known as a tough union bargainer and a man who can call on political officials for support during labor negotiations. His mentor is Cardinal John O'Connor, who supports him as "a man of integrity." Jesse Jackson is another supporter.

Rivera has been critical of both wealthy corporations and labor unions. Tax the rich, Rivera has insisted. But he also has said that some labor unions have become "fat" and see their objectives as "a business, not a mission or a cause." Rivera often liked to quote poet José Martí who wrote about "sailing against the wind." ∎

ventured far from the American Southwest. In New Rochelle, New York, the Chicano population had nearly doubled during the 1980s to 7,200 people in a city of 67,000.

Many found new jobs, homes, and lives in New Rochelle through the efforts of Antonio Valencia, 69, who was affectionately known as *padrino*, or the godfather. "He's here taking care of us, that's really what he is doing," said George Castellanos, the Hispanic liaison for the city school system.

In 1954, Valencia came to New Rochelle as a housekeeper for a former mayor and his wife. Valencia did not know a word of

English and felt isolated for years. Often tempted to return to Mexico, Valencia remained to search for "the opportunity to help my people." He raised funds at card parties and dances in New Rochelle to build a school in his native town in Mexico.

Valencia was widely known in New Rochelle for his efforts to increase Hispanic representation on local committees and to ease strained relations between his people and the police. "He is very concerned for his people," said Mayor Timothy Idoni. "He exemplifies what the city of New Rochelle needs in leadership." A beneficiary described Valencia's work: "He brings them to doctors. He gets them to court."

In the recession of 1992 Valencia and his helpers tried to aid the unemployed. Said storekeeper Juan Sandoval,

> They have no place to go. Many can't get jobs. We treat
> them for free when they don't have the money to buy. Its
> sad. We all come from the same region [of Mexico]. We're
> all connected somehow.

At a luncheon to honor Valencia, Jorge Montano, the Mexican ambassador to the United States, said, "You don't find that many people nowadays who are so generous but not looking for any benefit."

Hispanic Americans were a fourth of New York City's population. But the 896,763 Puerto Ricans were no longer a majority of the Hispanic American population, though they did constitute 80 percent of Hispanic Americans registered to vote. Spanish-speaking people had come from Mexico, most of the countries in the West Indies, and Central and South America. The number of Mexican Americans had grown from 60,000 in 1980 to an estimated 400,000 in 1992, and they had become the city's second-largest Hispanic group. Illegal aliens brought the total even higher.

People from the Dominican Republic numbered more than 330,000, and some owned restaurants, bodegas (stores), and taxicab fleets. Marlene Cintron, director of the Office of Latino Affairs for Mayor David Dinkins, was a Puerto Rican married to a Dominican. She stressed the need for cooperation among Hispanics:

> Those who understand real empowerment understand
> that we need to do it together.

C H A P T E R   4

AMERICANS FROM THE WEST INDIES

The West Indies are home to 13 independent countries as well as dependencies of the United States and European nations. The islands have a total population of about 34 million. Between 1980 and 1990, more people reached the United States from the West Indies than from all of Europe.

Emigrants have been drawn to a land of opportunity and education they watch on satellite TV or hear about from returning students. Said a Dominican newspaper editor,

> The elites of this country have always sent their children to be educated in the United States, and when they have returned, it has always been a triumphant return, looking good and speaking English. The message for the rest of us has been so well received it has assumed an almost demonic force. If you stay here like good Dominicans, you will be left behind.

In the 1980s small islands in the West Indies, such as Nevis and St. Kitts, lost one to two percent of their residents each year to the U.S. During the decade, the largest number of immigrants from the West Indies, a quarter of a million, came from the Dominican Republic. Jamaica sent 213,805, Haiti 140,163, and Guyana 95,374. Most newcomers settled in Baltimore, Miami, New York, and Boston.

Jamaica, a nation of 2,540,000, lost 9 percent of its people to the United States between 1980 and 1990, a higher percentage than any other country. Jamaicans constituted almost 3 percent of all immigrants who entered America during the decade. Many who emigrated were doctors, nurses, and teachers — a serious brain drain for a very poor country. Arrivals in the United States sent back enough money to have a positive impact on the Jamaican economy.

People from islands in the West Indies, such as Jamaica, Trinidad and Tobago, Antigua, Barbados, and some smaller islands, plus Guyana on the South American continent, amount to two million in the United States, and almost half live in New York City. Most enter the United States with a good education, and money and work skills, which they turn into business acumen.

After 20 years in America, West Indians earn more money than African Americans, just as white immigrants, after 20 years, earn more than native-born whites. Said Roy Hastic, president of the Caribbean-American Chamber of Commerce and Industry, Inc.,

> They give up their homes and their jobs to come here.
> When they get here, they know that they have to get a job
> and an education to survive.

West Indian enthusiasm for business is legendary. People bring investment habits learned in the West Indies and raise investment funds, which they call *susu*, from friends and family. Columbia University's Dr. Saskia Sassen examined this West Indian spirit in America:

> First generation immigrants will take any kind of job and
> do any kind of hard work. They are the greatest believers
> in the American dream. They think that through hard work
> anything can be achieved. They will work [in] two or three
> jobs to get the capitalization needed to open a small shop.

In 1992, the U.S. Embassy in the Dominican Republic interviewed more than 300 applicants for emigration each day. "People will leave everything behind for a chance of a job in the United States," reported the American consul general in Santo Domingo. Many first sail to the American Virgin Islands or Puerto Rico. An estimated 30,000 Dominicans each year land in Puerto Rico.

Since Fidel Castro took power in Cuba in 1959, opponents of Castro's form of communism have been welcomed to American shores because they were anticommunists and their flight embarrassed Castro. About a quarter of a million Cubans fled their homeland after an agreement was signed by the United States and Cuba in 1965. Between then and 1973, another quarter of a million of Castro's adversaries reached the United States by airlift.

In 1980, hundreds of Cubans fled to the United States by boat.

In 1980 thousands more left on boats that sailed from the Cuban port of Mariel to Key West, Florida. Within a few weeks 125,000 arrived to massive American media coverage. Many refugees were highly educated, middle-class foes of Castro. White business people and their families comprised 90 percent of the exodus. Cubans whose ancestors came from Africa, a quarter of the island's population, were less willing to abandon Castro, whom they felt fought racism.

In the first five months of 1992, 2,000 Cubans sailed to Florida, and American law enabled them to become legal residents almost upon arrival. They joined a million Cuban Americans already living on United States soil.

About two-thirds of all Cuban Americans have settled in Florida, and about a fifth in New Jersey and New York. Those in southern Florida sparked an economic boom.

Before 1980, a federal Cuban refugee program handed a billion and a half dollars to arriving Cubans along with medical care, and job and educational counseling. States then were asked to pick up some costs of the Cuban upkeep. This extraordinary government attention and largess to largely white Cubans has caused ill feeling on the part of African Americans in Florida.

Federal aid also has helped produce a Cuban upper class in the United States. In the 1980s Cuban American incomes rose four times as fast as other residents. Many joined Florida's middle class. By 1990, a third of all Cuban Americans were between 20 and 39 years of age. More than a third of all Cuban Americans earned more than $50,000 a year. As "Yucas," or Yuppy Cubans, they were upwardly mobile, bicultural, and bilingual.

Cuban Americans became the wealthiest Hispanic Americans, their median income almost double that of Puerto Ricans. Some elderly Cuban Americans or those in single parent families live below the poverty line. However, they still hold to traditional family values, religion, and language as they pursue America's material advantages.

Not all Cuban Americans though considered themselves foes of Castro. The sons and daughters of people who fled Castro, many of whom have been Americans for thirty or more years, often displayed little hatred toward Castro.

In keeping with its foreign policy, the United States government has consistently provided financial aid for other anticommunist refugees. For example, Nicaraguans who fled that country's Sandinista government were settled in California and Miami with U.S. aid. On the other hand, federal policy was used to refuse entry to people fleeing Haiti. Beginning in 1974, boatloads of Haitians tried to flee the brutal Duvalier dictatorship that dominated their poverty-stricken island. Even when their leaky boats managed to reach the shores of Florida, Haitians were seized and turned back. What awaited them, they swore, was jail, torture, and possibly death.

In January 1991, Father Jean-Bertrand Aristide, a Catholic priest, became the first popularly elected democratic ruler of Haiti. For a while emigration virtually stopped. But nine months later, in September, Aristide was overthrown and forced into exile by the Haitian military. As a new military dictatorship assumed power, Haitians began a new flight to the United States.

Fleeing military dictatorships, Haitians were halted by the U.S. Coast Guard, and most were returned to Haiti.

The Bush administration said that these boat people were not truly political refugees, but "economic refugees" seeking a better life. On that basis, the State Department ordered the U.S. Coast Guard to intercept Haitian craft at sea and, without hearings, return people to Haiti. Only 2 percent of Haitians won the right to remain in America. By the first half of 1992, the Coast Guard had halted 28,000 Haitians at sea and sent them home to an unknown fate.

In 1991 an incident in the Caribbean highlighted the difference between how the U.S. treated Cuban boat people and how Haitian boat people were treated. An old wooden craft loaded with 161 fleeing Haitians rescued two Cubans floating on an inner tube raft. As their boat headed toward Miami, it was halted by the U.S. Coast Guard. The Americans gave refuge to the Cubans but not the Haitians.

RUSSIAN AND IRISH IMMIGRANTS

Migrations of people from Europe to America rose in the 1980s, often spurred by political turmoil, ethnic or religious persecution, or joblessness at home. Many immigrants left the disintegrating Soviet Empire, particularly Jews who feared for their lives. In 1990, Russian Jewish novelist Irina Ginzburg wrote:

Russian Jewish immigrants to America meet with a social worker in Boston, Massachusetts.

> You cannot imagine what is happening in Moscow — panic, terror, fear. People are talking about one thing only: how and where to go, to hide when they come to kill you.
>
> Many Jews have already moved to the homes of Russian friends....But will this save them?

The Jewish emigration from Russia increased faster than the United States could process arrivals. In 1985 the United States issued 400 immigrant visas to Russians, and by 1990, that had more than tripled to 1,300.

Soviet permits were issued if the Jewish emigrants agreed to state their ultimate destination was Israel. However, only 7 percent of the Jews who left the USSR settled in Israel. The rest chose the United States, said one, because it was "a fairy-tale story." Some Russian immigrants, surprised to find the harsh reality of crime and poverty in the United States, returned to their homeland.

Russian Jewish immigrants to America were welcomed by Jewish American relief societies which had aided immigrants of earlier times. Many settled in the growing Russian community in Brighton Beach, Brooklyn, New York.

By 1990, the number of Russian immigrants who came as visitors increased tenfold over those who had arrived as visitors five years earlier. Those requesting asylum in the same period soared from less than a hundred to more than 1,800. Others stayed on illegally.

In 1991, 61,000 Russians, mostly Jews, were offered refugee status as oppressed people. The waiting list for such visas had grown to 500,000 by 1992. In the 1990s a fourth wave of Russians had begun to leave their country, and most were not Jews. Many of the estimated 30,000 illegal Russian residents of the United States in 1991 and 1992 were Christians although some were Muslims. They came on visitors' visas and planned to stay illegally when these expired. These Russians represented a cross section of their society — jewelers, sailors, actresses, army deserters, would-be fashion models, and mothers with children. In 1992, photographers, environmentalists, microbiologists, and rock musicians arrived.

Russian attorneys have entered the United States as interns in American law firms. Ms. Paliashvili, a Soviet Georgian lawyer, took a job in Chicago. She left to get away from the ethnic conflict in her homeland and to get "a kind of look from the other side and see things from a long-term perspective." Yelena Barikhnovskaya completed six months of study with the Lawyers Committee for Human Rights in New York City. She plans to return to St. Petersburg and begin a similar committee.

Not all newcomers have found work on their professional level. Some have taken work as housemaids or laborers. Limpopo, a three-member male Russian rock band, composed of a balalaika player, guitar player, and trombone player, arrived with tourist visas and played on street corners for a living.

Anatoly Belilovsky came to the United States at 15 in 1976. He graduated from Brooklyn Technical High School, Princeton University, and the University of Connecticut School of Medicine. He became a pediatrician and settled in Brighton Beach, where with his mother, also a doctor, they soon had 5,000 patients, of which 4,000 were Russian immigrants.

Treating immigrant patients was difficult, Dr. Belilovsky found, because Soviet doctors had not given vaccinations or good prenatal care to their patients. Many mothers were afraid to have their children receive vaccinations required by American schools.

In the ten years ending in 1991, 206,000 people left Ireland, about 6 percent of the total population. Most were men and women in their twenties from the island's west coast. Journalist Deaglan de Breadun of the Dublin *Times* visited Carna, Ireland, and found "20 to 30 people leaving each year, from the 19-25 age group, mainly for Boston, New York, and Chicago." Many "had nice little jobs in factories," he found, and sought adventure and better jobs in America. Had they remained at home instead of emigrating, Breadun estimated, Ireland's jobless rate would have doubled. About three-quarters of the departing Irish came to the United States, and some 90,000 arrived as illegal immigrants.

Young women took jobs as waitresses, or they took care of children. Other young men and women, including many with high school degrees, came as students and then stayed on illegally. Francis Vardy, an expert on Irish immigration said,

> There is something in the Irish attitude that says, "I belong in America." They don't consider themselves foreigners. They consider the U.S. to be the 33rd county of Ireland.

The Irish immigration began to slow with the economic recession in the United States in the 1990s. Many in construction or other work returned to Ireland to wait out the economic storms. "Better to be unemployed at home," said a returning immigrant.

CHAPTER 6

ASIAN AMERICANS

Though comprising only 3 percent of the population in the 1990 census, Asian Americans are the fastest-growing U.S. minority. The makeup of the the Asian American population has changed dramatically since 1960 when it was 52 percent Japanese, 27 percent Chinese, 20 percent Filipino, 1 percent Asian Indian, and 1 percent Korean. By 1985, Asian Americans were as follows: 21 percent Chinese, 21 percent Filipino, 12 percent Vietnamese, 15 percent Japanese, 11 percent Korean, 10 percent Asian Indian, 4 percent Laotian, and 3 percent Cambodian.

The 1990 census placed the Asian American median household income at $36,784, when the national income median was $30,056. Although this indicated higher salaries for Asian Americans, these data do not take into account the fact that Asian American families had more wage earners than other families. Many Asian American family members work together, often in small retail businesses.

A higher income for Asian Americans is also explained by the fact that more than one in three Asian Americans have college degrees compared to one in five other Americans. High income, however, was not evenly spread among Asian Americans. About 12 percent live below the poverty line compared to 10 percent for white Americans. In Rhode Island, more than 25 percent of all Asian Americans lived in poverty, and 13 percent were unemployed.

Asian Americans have begun to edge ahead of most Americans in education. Among those age 25 and older, 82 percent have completed high school, compared to 80 percent for whites and less for other Americans. Some 39 percent of Asian Americans have completed four years of college, compared to 22 percent for whites and less for others. Almost twice the percentage of Asian Americans have completed a year of graduate school compared to whites.

However, educational attainment does not always mean a higher income. Asian American high school graduates earn only 79

Asian immigrants to America in the 1990s are often better educated than other Americans.

percent of what white high school graduates do, and Asian American college graduates earn 90 percent of what white college graduates do.

Half of all Asian Americans live in cities, and almost half live in the suburbs. Only 5 percent of Asian Americans live in rural areas of the U.S.

In 1988, about 80 percent of Vietnamese American voters were registered Republicans. In 1989 Sinchan Siv, a Vietnamese refugee, became President Bush's principal liaison for ethnic and minority affairs.

However, some Asian Americans who have lived in the United States for a decade or more, disagree with Republican policies. In Arlington, Virginia, Vietnamese store owners complained that President Bush's response to the recession had favored large rather than small businesses. Asian American parents rebelled against cutting funds for English as a Second Language classes. Asian American parents united with others to defeat a bill that would make English Maryland's official language.

Asian American women began to shed the inferior status imposed on them in their homelands. In 1992, Ming Chau, president of the Organization for Pan-Asian American Women, found Indochinese women, long hesitant to talk about problems, were beginning to use their new freedom in America. She said, "We are politically unsophisticated still. But to us, freedom is this very activism we're now discovering."

Japan's huge industrial growth cut down on Japanese emigration. The result is that 72 percent of Japanese Americans in 1980 were third *(Sansei)* or fourth *(Yonsei)* generation Americans, far more familiar with English than Japanese. Those Japanese who did come to the United States in the 1980s arrived in families and planned to stay. Many were skilled workers and educated men and women well prepared for jobs in a technological society.

The Chinese American community also has been changed by recent arrivals. Chinese Americans, only 237,000 in 1960, in 20 years numbered 812,000. In those 20 years the Chinese American community changed from 61 percent American-born to 63 percent foreign-born. Most newcomers settled in cities, 60 percent in California and New York. New York's Chinatown suddenly expanded to become the home for 100,000 people.

In his book *Strangers from a Different Shore*, a history of Asian Americans written in 1990, author Ronald Takaki found crowded Chinatowns housed 51 percent of Chinese Americans. They were largely foreign-born, and lacked education and a knowledge of English. Men worked for low wages as waiters, dishwashers, janitors, or cooks. Women worked 12 hours a day, six days a week in crowded sweatshops, and some even brought their babies to work.

Since English is the stepping-stone to higher salaries, many poor Chinese Americans tried to learn English in special classes. But spending long hours at sewing machines leaves one little time for attending classes and studying a foreign language. People who held professional jobs in China found the language barrier restricted them to only unskilled jobs.

Desperation sometimes drove young men to join street gangs that extorted funds from Chinatown business people. Asked why he chose a life of crime, a young Chinese American answered, "To keep from being a waiter all my life."

Some sweatshop workers joined the International Ladies Garment Workers Union (ILGWU). In 1982, Chinese American union leader Alice Tse said, "Chinese workers are people, too! We should receive equal treatment."

However, in Monterey Park, California, Chinese from Taiwan and Hong Kong created the first American suburban Chinatown. In 1980 the town elected its first Chinese American mayor, Lilly Chen. Monterey Park's bank accounts averaged $25,000 for each resident. Chinese Americans owned two-thirds of the town land and boasted their own doctors, theaters, churches, and lawyers.

East Indians in America, only 10,000 in 1945, numbered over one-half million people by 1985. Most were English-speaking, educated professionals.

More than a third lived in cities in the Northeast, though some others, mostly single men, were farmers in California. In 1990 almost

In 1987, there were 52,266 Asian Indian-owned businesses, such as these in Brooklyn, New York.

half of the employed East Indian American men were listed as managers and professionals, including 25,000 doctors and dentists, 40,000 engineers, and 20,000 scientists. Others operated pizza parlors, travel agencies, and restaurants. East Indians owned more than a fourth of all U.S. motels.

In 1975, the Association of Indians in America asked the U.S. Civil Rights Commission to protect them from discrimination since their appearance sets them apart from whites. Though the majority of Indians are educated professionals, the league warned, many others faced comparison to "Korean and Japanese immigrants." The U.S. Census Bureau by 1990 agreed to reclassify people from India as "Asian Indian" rather than "white/Caucasian."

By 1980, Pakistanis were publishing about 100 periodicals, and there were 200 Pakistani American social and self-help organizations thriving mostly in major cities. The Muslim Students of America and the Pakistan Students' Association attracted more than a thousand people to their annual conventions.

In August 1990, Pakistani American residents along Brooklyn, New York's Coney Island Avenue held the first Pakistan Day Festival to celebrate the 40,000 of their fellow countrymen and women who lived in the U.S. The theme was voter registration, and the festival attracted 10,000 New Yorkers of every religion and nationality.

Festival organizer Syed Faz Haq, a bank clerk, recalled that when he arrived in the U.S. in 1971 "there were only a handful of Pakistanis....We've come of age as a community." He added,

> It is in our best interests as a community to vote; it is a must. We have many things to offer as a community. We know our rights as Americans; we must do our duty as Americans as well.

Though the festival date was selected to celebrate Pakistan's independence in 1947, it was also picked, said another festival organizer, "to establish our independence politically as a community." "I'm Proud to Be a Pakistani" buttons enjoyed a brisk sale.

About 60 percent of Asian Americans, or more than four million, live in the western states, most or 39 percent in California. Almost a million live in the Los Angeles area. Some 29 percent of San Francisco's inhabitants came from Asia, the highest percentage of

Chinatown in San Francisco, California, is home to a large population of Chinese Americans. In San Francisco County, 29 percent of the residents in 1990 came from Asia.

any county in mainland United States. In Hawaii 62 percent of the state's population is from Asia. New York City has more than one-half million Asian American residents, more than San Francisco.

In the workplace, Asian Americans often found they could rise only so far in management positions and faced discrimination because of their "limited English proficiency." Others had been stereotyped as being unaggressive or too technically oriented to assume higher command in corporations. Asian Americans were underrepresented (8 percent) as officials and managers when compared to other Americans (12 percent). A *Wall Street Journal* article stated, "The same companies that pursue them [Asian Americans] for technical jobs often shun them when filling managerial and executive positions."

A Civil Rights Commission report in 1992 criticized schools for having too few teachers who speak Asian languages. The result is that children of Asian immigrants are "encountering more educational difficulties than earlier waves [of immigrants]."

In the 1980s, Korean, Chinese, and Vietnamese Americans focused their economic resources within their communities. Filipinos, Japanese, and Asian Indians integrated their economic activities with other Americans.

The Korean grocery store became a fixture in many urban centers in the 1980s. About 78 percent of those who managed the groceries held college degrees. These enterprises attracted Korean American men with degrees in city planning or mechanical engineering who could not find jobs elsewhere. Yun Pang quit work at an American insurance company. He met a Korean born in the U.S. who spoke perfect English and had years of experience. When this man told Pang he was regularly bypassed in favor of whites at promotion time, Pang decided it was time to work for himself.

In 1988, in San Jose, California, the 10 percent Vietnamese American population owned 40 percent of the city's businesses. "There's a new vitality downtown, and it's the Vietnamese who have made it what it is today," said Doanh Chau, director of the Vietnamese Chamber of Commerce.

Intermarriage between ethnic groups, such as this marriage between a European American groom and Chinese American bride, are becoming more common.

Both integration and diversity coexisted in Asian American communities. In California, in 1980, the rate of intermarriage for Japanese was 32 percent, Filipinos 24 percent, Asian Indians 23 percent, Koreans 19 percent, Vietnamese 15 percent, and Chinese 14 percent. Yet many Asian Americans proudly embraced their own diversity, studied their ancient cultures, and rejoiced in their traditional life. Their children studied Asian American history at colleges and benefited from bilingual education.

Integration into mainstream American culture, however, was more difficult. At the University of California at Los Angeles, Ronald Takaki found grafitti that reinforced stereotypes: "UCLA stands for University of Caucasians Living Among Asians," "Stop the Chinese Before They Flunk You Out!" He cited bigots who warned about "a large influx of third-world people, which could be potentially disruptive of our whole Judeo-Christian heritage." Anti-Asian stereotypes, he believed, also were promoted in *Rambo* movies and films about the Vietnam War.

Takaki found large pockets of poverty and inadequate social service programs among Asian Americans. Such pockets developed particularly among elderly Japanese, Filipino, and Chinese Americans. Takaki has also discovered a new spirit among Asian immigrants:

[A]ll Asian Americans — Chinese, Japanese, Koreans, Filipinos, Asian Indians, and Southeast Asians — are standing up this time....Though they represent diverse communities, Asian Americans have come together and joined their voices in protest.

CHAPTER 7

ASIANS AND THE AMERICAN DREAM

Largely through immigration, the number of Asian immigrants has more than doubled from 3.5 million in 1980 to over 7 million in 1990. Three out of four new Asians in California were immigrants. Most came from Korea, Iran, China, Taiwan, Cambodia, India, Pakistan, Laos, and the Philippines.

Filipinos composed the single largest group of Asians in the United States in 1990. More than 600,000 had arrived from the Philippines in the twenty years following 1965, most of them in family groups. Many fled human rights violations and the corruption that marked the Ferdinand Marcos dictatorship. Newcomers included doctors, nurses, attorneys, teachers, and other professionals.

Most Filipinos came to the United States seeking decent jobs and intending to stay. "In the United States hard work is rewarded. In the Philippines, it is part of the struggle to survive," said an accountant. By 1990, many Filipino doctors practiced in the U.S.

As of 1993, 50,000 Filipino American doctors practiced medicine in the United States.

However, some who were lawyers, dentists, and engineers in the Philippines had to take jobs as file clerks, aides, and secretaries in the United States. Many found a labor market that paid them half of what it paid whites in the same occupations.

Many Chinese entered the United States as part of a "chain-reaction" immigration. Chinese youths who attended American colleges in the 1960s stayed on as immigrants under the preference category for professional jobs permitted by the 1965 immigration law. Then, by applying the family preference provisions of the act, they brought over their wives, children, parents, and other relatives. These immigrants then brought their children and other relatives, and so the chain reaction grew.

More women than men arrived from China, and most people were from cities. Some had fled Chinese communism during the persecutions of the Cultural Revolution. Others had left Taiwan to escape the oppressive Chiang Kai-shek dictatorship. Chin Moy Lee, who arrived in 1968 from China, said,

> There was hot running water, cold water, and even warm air. The water in the village countryside was filthy....Any place with "clean water" must be like "the sky above the sky." America is "heaven."

Chinese immigrants also found overcrowding, hard work, disease, unemployment, and poor housing in America. Salaries for Chinese American men in San Francisco were 68 percent of what whites received. In New York City, they were 56 percent of what whites were paid. Chinese American women made even less — 36 percent of what white women were paid in San Francisco and 44 percent of what whites earned in New York City. Unemployment among Chinese immigrants was double that of whites, and suicides were higher than the national average. More than a third of the people who settled in New York's Chinatown lived below the poverty line.

However by 1983, Korean Americans owned three-quarters of the greengroceries in New York City. Running a grocery requires hard work and long hours by each family member. Although some groceries claimed profits of close to $100,000 a year, most made between $17,000 and $35,000 a year. These earnings had to be divided among many family members who shared the labor.

In the quarter century that ended in 1985 the Korean American population soared from 10,000 to one-half million people. Due largely to language problems, about 80 percent worked within their ethnic communities at low-paying jobs. One said of his American experience, "It is work, work, work."

With a wife at work in one place and a husband in another, life in America challenged traditional Korean families. "The family here is too loose," complained Tran Xuan Quang, a mother who arrived in Oakland, California, expecting her children to take care of her. Instead, she reported, "[They] threw me out of the house."

Other Korean Americans found life less painful and more rewarding. In addition to successful shopkeepers, there were also a number of doctors and other professionals who were able to resume their careers in the United States.

By 1992, Asians were reaching these shores at the rate of 52,000 a year. Most were boat people fleeing oppression. Some were Amerasian children born to Asian mothers and American servicemen who had been sent to Asia to fight communism.

One of the receiving stations for the newcomers was Park Warren in Arlington, Virginia. Successive waves of Indochinese refugees moved into crowded apartments that often lacked heat and water. Some were able to "move up" into cheap houses in Fairfax, Virginia, or Rockville, Maryland, where jobs were available in service industries or in the factories on Route 270. *The Economist* reported,

> The Vietnamese have set up more than 600 businesses
> around Washington, run with typical industriousness. On
> Saturday mornings the narrow aisles of their grocery
> stores are jammed with Vietnamese women buying herbs
> and vegetables familiar from home.

In nearby Washington, D.C., Vietnamese Americans established their own newspaper and a cable television program, and provided classes in English. Cambodian immigrants remained longer in Park Warren than other Asian groups.

Along with success came new challenges. Life in America was difficult for the Vietnamese families who had fled after the U.S. pulled out of South Vietnam. For example, the Vietnamese were accustomed to arranged marriages and to women who were kept dependent on their husbands for income. In the 1980s, about 40 percent of Vietnamese American women joined the labor market, some eagerly. Said one woman, "I can work! Someone will hire me here."

Vietnamese men had to learn not to feel insecure if their wives took jobs. With encouragement, some men began to help at home. Said one, "She never tells me that I should help her, but I think because she is working like me, too, I should give her a hand."

Refugees from Vietnam, like others, often had to take low-paying jobs. One teacher admitted he had to take jobs as a

> bricklayer, carpenter, clerk-typist, salesman, truck driver,
> delivery man. I felt frustrated and depressed because I
> had social status and possessions in Vietnam. Here I
> didn't have anything.

Other professionals found their niche in America. In 1988, the city council of Westminster, California, named a prosperous business area "Little Saigon" because Vietnamese residents shopped and hired services in Vietnamese. In Orange County, California, Vietnamese were doctors and dentists, and Chinese who came from Vietnam ran groceries, restaurants, and supermarkets.

The Vietnam War produced another refugee group when U.S. forces entered Laos, a mountainous land between Thailand and Vietnam. America's Laotian allies arrived seeking sanctuary. However, many Laotians had lived as independent, landowning farmers or by hunting and fishing, and they found adjustment to the United States trying and difficult. "It is easier to move the mountains than get used to American culture," said one Laotian.

One refugee compared the jungle in Laos to "another kind of jungle" in America — "a technological and bureaucratic jungle." Many Laotian Americans took low-paying jobs or joined welfare rolls. Others did well. Kimmakone Siharath, who said in Laos he would be a farmer, majored in genetics at the University of California at Berkeley. He applied for U.S. citizenship but said,

> No matter how long you are here in America, you will
> always be an Asian, always an outsider, not an American.

The Mien and Hmong were two ethnic groups from Laos who also fled to America. In the United States, the Mien settled in Portland, Oregon, and Seattle, Washington, and in Sacramento, Oakland, San Jose, and Long Beach, California. Some 20,000 Hmong settled in Fresno, California, others in Seattle, Washington, and in Minnesota farm towns.

These two ethnic groups had been independent farmers, and 70 percent of both peoples had no knowledge of a written language. They experienced difficulties in adjusting to stoves, toilets, telephone bills, and welfare forms. First they had to be taught to read and write in their own language before they learned English. They also had to learn new American farming methods. With a jobless rate that sometimes soared to 90 percent, thousands barely survived. "We are not even farmers anymore," said one Hmong, "we are just unemployed soldiers."

Many Hmong and Mien faced ethnic hatred. "Racism is like a

wall," said one Hmong, "You cannot break through it." However, young Hmong were learning English, and a few entered colleges.

Cambodians had been drawn into the Vietnam War in 1971 when President Nixon ordered the bombing of enemy supply lines in their country. In 1975 Pol Pot's Khmer Rouge seized Cambodia, renamed it Kampuchea, and began a reign of terror that took an estimated two million lives. The Khmer Rouge singled out the educated classes, including doctors, lawyers, and teachers, for destruction. Then hundreds of thousands fled to Thailand when Vietnamese troops invaded Cambodia in 1978 and overthrew the Pol Pot government.

By 1990, over 100,000 Cambodian refugees had settled in the United States. Many were women who had lost their husbands in the "killing fields." Most were poor peasants haunted by harrowing captivity, shattered lives, and the death of loved ones. The United States became a haven of opportunity. "We want a chance to become part of this country," said one. "It is a chance for a new life. But inside, the memories are still there." Many refugees brought their nightmares and emotional turmoil.

Cambodians also experienced anguish as they stepped from an ancient farming society into industrial America. Sathaya Tor had worked in a Khmer Rouge labor camp for four years and escaped to Thailand at age 12. In 1988, he enrolled at Stanford University in California, the only Cambodian American except for the janitor. He described his cultural suffering to Ronald Takaki:

> In a way, to be assimilated in another culture, you have to
> give up your own culture. With one foot in each culture,
> the wider you have to spread your legs, the more you
> could lose your balance. I'm at a point in my life where for
> the first time I feel vulnerable, and its scary.

Cambodians, such as Chanthou Sam who arrived in 1975 at age 12, accepted the challenges of American life. At age 18, Sam won enough scholastic honors and admiration from her fellow students to be elected Rose Festival Princess in Portland, Oregon. She wanted to become an accountant, but her American ambitions clashed with her ancient cultural values. Sam said,

> A Cambodian woman is supposed to sit at home, cook,
> and clean house. I want to be somebody. I want my own
> job, house, and car before I marry. I want to be independent.
> It is very hard to be caught in the clash of cultures.

East Indian immigrants were equally divided between men and women. "We were already assimilated in India before we came here," said one.

Most East Indian Americans arrived in the United States to stay and have sought citizenship. However, many have found America a wrenching change. Dr. S. Patel arrived in 1967 as part of an arranged marriage and planned to return home with her husband. In the following ten years she had a son and graduated from medical school. But in 1990 she thought of returning to India.

> Why? Because there is too much individualism here in
> America....In India, children take care of their parents.
> This doesn't happen in this country. So there's a price to
> be paid for coming here. The family isn't as close here.

Before Pakistan declared its independence from India in 1947, few people from that country entered the United States. Between 1965 and 1970 about 2,000 Pakistanis arrived. After East Pakistan (Bangladesh) and West Pakistan divided in 1971, immigration rose to 2,000 a year. Most newcomers were college-educated or professionally trained urban men. Ten percent were doctors, and ten percent were engineers. As soon as a Pakistani husband in the United States earned enough to provide food, clothing, shelter, and education, he was expected to send for his family. Pakistani American networks helped new arrivals find jobs and adjust to the new country.

The family structure in Pakistan was dominated by the husband or father. Women were expected to remain in the home rather than work. In America these traditions began to crumble as wives took jobs.

The demands and tensions of Americanization affected East Indian families profoundly. Newly arrived parents spoke their original languages while their children quickly learned English at school. The rapid assimilation of children led to stress and conflicts with parents.

CHAPTER 8

NATIVE AMERICANS

The 1990 U.S. census report indicates that the number of people who called themselves Native Americans had tripled since 1960. Cherokee sociologist Russell Thornton of the University of California explained this increase:

> There were many people who were ashamed of their
> Indian past, so they hid it. But a lot of people who went
> the assimilationist route have come back. And the tribes
> have been enjoying a renaissance.

Identification of Native Americans with their heritage stemmed from a number of factors. Growing concern with modern ecological disasters has revived appreciation for the Native American respect for the environment. Prejudice against Indians has faded in recent decades. Once portrayed as bloodthirsty and aggressive, today Native Americans are seen as proud people with meaningful cultures.

Donald E. Pelotte, 46, from Gallup, New Mexico, of Abnaki Indian and French Canadian descent, was appointed the first Native American Catholic bishop in 1986. In 1992, he said of his people's legacy:

> When I was growing up in Maine, few Native Americans
> here knew much about our traditions. But I am amazed at
> how much has been recovered in just the last 10 years.
> Our struggle to return to our traditions is the same
> struggle of many Native Americans around the country.

The drive to recapture Native American cultures has been taken up by children as well as adults. Jennifer Bates told how her nine-year-old son had taken an interest in Northern Miwok dance.

> It's nice, knowing that we're not pushing it on him. He
> wanted to dance and make his cape. It's up to us to keep
> things going, and if we don't, it's gone.

Ethnic pride also encouraged many Indians to affirm their heritage. In California, for example, various nations, such as the Chippewas and the Cherokees, have united in city clubs. One authority described this as "the formation of an intertribal ethic, a pan-Indian ethic." He attributed it to "cultural doubt" by people who now wish to abandon a white America for "something they can draw strength from."

During the 1980s, the Native American population soared by 38 percent to an estimated 1,900,000 people. Most of this growth took place in states such as Oklahoma, Arizona, and California, each with more than 200,000 Indian residents.

Some 388,000 Native Americans lived on 314 reservations, with a thousand or more on each. The Navajo Reservation and Trust was the largest, with 143,400 residents.

Native American nations review applicants for membership, and each nation has different requirements. Some accept only those who can prove an ancestry that is at least half Native American, while other nations accept men and women with any Indian ancestors.

Participation at traditional powwows increased steadily as Native Americans returned to their roots. In New York City, the National Alliance of Native Americans and the Northeast Native American Association are groups composed mostly of African Americans with Indian blood who wish to explore this dimension of their biological legacy in the 1990s.

In Denver, Colorado, Wallace Coffee, a Comanche, organized the Denver Indian Center as a church to preserve traditional Indian worship. He said, "Many of our people grew up with a sense that there was something missing. In the past 15 years, we've seen a strong return to the [Indian] value system and traditions." John Homer, born a Chickasaw in Oklahoma, was adopted by whites who changed his name. At 44, he assumed his Chickasaw name, saying, "It was time for me to reclaim my heritage." He became the head of the Living Waters Indian Ministry Christian Church for Native Americans. Homer argued,

> For a long time, Native Americans have been told, "If you can pass, then do it." We need to be telling our people, "It's okay that you're an Indian. Make your presence known."

Despite the rise of identification with their ancient civilizations, half of Native Americans in the 1990s married non-Indians.

The Native American legacy spurred a cultural renaissance in many communities, creating more jobs and new businesses on reservations. Indian art and tourism have become increasingly popular among all Americans.

In 1992 Salish and Kutenai Indians opened this $6.3 million resort on Flathead Lake in Montana.

The number of Native American-owned businesses increased by two-thirds in the five years ending in 1987 — at a time when all American businesses increased only 14 percent. "Indians see self-employment as a viable opportunity," reported Steven Stallings, president of the National Center for American Indian Enterprise Development in Mesa, Arizona. He sought to build businesses that could support reservations. Whites usually spend 85 percent of their money within their communities, but Native Americans spend up to 90 percent of their income outside their reservations. Stallings sought to attract outside employers who will build retail and service businesses and "create a revolving economy on the reservation."

The Lagunas in New Mexico owned several enterprises, including Laguna Industries, which employs 350 people and serves the Department of Defense and such large corporations as Raytheon and Martin Marietta. Laguna workers produced a communications shelter used by the U.S. Army during the Gulf War. However, defense contracts offered little security in the post-cold war era.

Training for the Lagunas was administered by white retirees who served as supervisors until the Lagunas learned to take over each production operation. The Laguna Industries experiment, however, did not solve other problems. Unemployment remained at 35 percent, and poor housing conditions and alcoholism still plagued families. Said one resident,

In North Carolina, Cherokees run a successful bingo casino.

> We need to develop more. People leave the reservation to get jobs. If there were jobs here, they'd stay.

Some 113 Native American reservations in 1992 allowed some form of gambling such as bingo, and some individual casinos drew as many as 5,000 people a week and hired 140 employees. Though casinos often raised

money for economic development, they also resulted in increased alcoholism and other vices.

Many Native American enterprises are run by couples and their children. The Zuni nation revived ancient crafts by opening two craft stores, one in their pueblo in New Mexico and one on San Francisco's posh Union Street. Their most popular items were fetishes, carvings of animals that bring good luck.

Progress in business ownership for Native Americans did not eliminate reservation poverty and the problems associated with it. Oklahoma, with the largest Indian population in America in 1990, had a Native American median household income of $18,051 and a poverty rate of 29 percent. In Arizona, Utah, and New Mexico the Native American poverty rate exceeds 40 percent.

U.S. Senator Ben Nighthorse Campbell

Ben Nighthorse Campbell was born in 1933 in California. His father was Northern Cheyenne. Ben grew up with a foot in two cultures, one Indian and one white. A member of the U.S. Olympic judo team in 1964, he remained a fighter of sorts all his life. He also raised cattle on his ranch with his wife Linda and their two children.

In 1982, Campbell won election to the Colorado State Legislature. While proudly wearing a ponytail, he fought for farmers and ranchers on water rights issues in the legislature.

Elected to Congress from Colorado in 1986, Campbell won more votes than any other Democratic candidate for the House of Representatives and became the only person with Native American ancestry then in Congress. "Indians have never had any political clout and very little voice in congressional matters," he said.

During his first term, Campbell felt his greatest achievement was the passage by Congress of his bill to settle Colorado Ute Indian water rights and consequently pave the way for construction of an Ute water project. He also backed a 1990 Colorado law to limit the terms of state and federal officeholders and dramatically announced he only intended to serve four terms himself. By then, the congressman had only token opposition.

Campbell refused to run for an open U.S. Senate seat because this would mean having to raise money from lobbyists. Nevertheless, in 1992 he became the first Native American elected to the U.S. Senate. ■

CHAPTER 9

AFRICAN AMERICANS

The 30 million African Americans in 1990 constituted 12.1 percent of the United States population. Census bureau officials have acknowledged this statistic may represent an undercount of as much as 5 percent. What is clear is that the number of African Americans had grown by 13.2 percent since the 1980 census, higher than the national average of 9.8 percent. This growth included 2 million immigrants who came mostly from West Indian nations. African American populations were growing in the same places white populations were growing — in the four most populous states (California, New York, Texas, and Florida) and in the suburbs.

The southern states remained home to 53 percent of the African American population. Many lived in "Black Belt" counties in Georgia, Mississippi, Alabama, and South Carolina which had the lowest per capita incomes in the country and the highest unemployment rates. Others lived in poverty-stricken urban ghettos. The county with the largest number of African Americans is Cook County, Illinois, where Blacks number about 1.3 million people.

In recent years, the poverty level for African Americans and the gap between them and white Americans has increased. In the 1980s, as the rich became richer, the poor did worse than they had earlier. The median income for white families rose to a record high of $31,435 in 1989, but the median income for black families remained at $19,758. In other words, Blacks earned 63 cents for every dollar whites earned, a one cent increase in a decade.

Black unemployment was double the white rate, and the rate among young black men sometimes soared as high as 50 percent. Half of black children lived below the poverty line, many in single parent families.

In 1990, when the average life expectancy in the United States was 75.3 years, the life expectancy for an African American man was 64.8 years. In other words, the average black male could expect

Filmmaker Spike Lee wearing his Malcolm X *hat in 1992.*

to die before he could collect social security. Blacks are twice as likely as whites to die before their first birthday and three times as likely as whites to die of AIDS.

However, between the 1960s and the 1990s, millions of African Americans climbed into the middle class. There were more black actors, scholars, models, physicians, bankers, and computer programmers than ever before. In 1991 alone, black film directors produced 19 movies, more than in the ten previous years. Filmmaker Spike Lee became a household name. By the 1990s, African American women novelists Alice Walker and Toni Morrison had won coveted Pulitzer Prizes. However, Toni Morrison said, "At no moment in my life have I ever felt as though I were an American."

In 1965, 19.5 percent of African Americans held white-collar jobs, and by 1985, the figure had more than doubled to 41 percent. Individuals were increasingly able to leave cities for suburbs. But this created new problems for inner-city neighborhoods. Ghetto life suffered new blows when leaders and people with capital pulled up and left. Neighborhoods became poorer, weaker, and more isolated.

Pulitzer Prize-winning novelist Toni Morrison.

The rising desperation of ghetto life was reflected in a frighteningly new statistic. More young African American men died from guns wielded by other Blacks than by any other cause.

Poverty was not always a matter of being jobless. Even people who worked, often at part-time jobs, lived with hunger. Kathryn Edin, a sociologist with the Russell Sage Foundation, interviewed single mothers in Boston, Chicago, San Antonio, Charleston, and Todd County, Minnesota. The main problem, she found, was

....that people can't live on the kinds of jobs they're able to get. With the work skills they have and the wages they can command in today's economy, they simply can't earn enough to meet their basic needs. The moms I talk to call it the "$5-an-hour-ghetto."...

Nevertheless, the ghetto has produced music that spanned the globe. Rap's insistent beats and unruly lyrics told how young African Americans saw their problems. By the 1990s, rap had imitators in Mexico, Brazil, Trinidad, England, France, Russia, Czechoslovakia, Poland, Hungary, India, China, and Japan. In 1988, LL Cool J gave a rap concert in Africa at the Ivory Coast capital of Abidjan that had 2,000 people dancing in the aisles and on chairs.

LL Cool J is a popular rap artist in the U.S. and around the world.

When middle-class African Americans in the 1980s entered professions such as journalism, they found that whites had unusual expectations of them. Black reporters were usually assigned to cover ghetto stories and rarely regular news. However, a black Florida

---

Kwanzaa

Maulana Ron Karenga, a political activist in California, created a unique cultural holiday in 1966 for people of African descent. He called it Kwanzaa, which in Swahili means "first fruits of the harvest." He saw it as a celebration of African culture and values, and selected elements from different African harvest festivals.

Kwanzaa is celebrated the last seven days of December. Part of the ceremony involves the lighting of black, red, and green candles in homes and community centers. Each day of Kwanzaa enunciates a basic principle of African culture, such as family unity, self-determination, collective responsibility, economic cooperation, restoration of traditional greatness, creativity, and renewed faith "in our people, our parents, our teachers, our leaders."

Eric and Kathleen Copage and their three-year-old son Evan were among an estimated 5 million Americans who celebrated Kwanzaa by 1990. Eric wanted Evan to learn about African Americans who devoted themselves to their community:

> I wanted him to understand that through tenacity, hard work, and purposefulness — all of which are grounded in the African and African American ethos — blacks have flourished as well as survived. And I wanted to train Evan to look for opportunity and to prepare for it.

In 1991, Eric Copage wrote a book, *Kwanzaa: An African American Celebration of Culture and Cooking* (Morrow, New York), for his family and his community. ■

journalist found that if he did not furnish news stories that showed ghetto people in a good light, nobody would.

Some black people left urban areas for less populated states, such as Montana, North Dakota, South Dakota, Idaho, Vermont, New Hampshire, or Maine, where they were a distinct minority. In 1989, African American incomes were on a national average 63 percent of white incomes, but in Montana black incomes were 87 percent of white incomes. The rate in North Dakota was 89 percent, in Maine 94 percent, and in Vermont 96 percent.

African American Gwen Kircher lived in Worden, Montana, where whites outnumbered blacks by 400 to one (2,000 out of 800,000). "Where there is prejudice here, it's based on ignorance not hate," she said. "And that's a whole lot easier to overcome." She joked about the local bigots:

They dislike the Indians first, and then come the
Mexicans. By the time they get around to us, they are
just too tired.

In Montana, Kircher faced only one racial incident. During a dispute, a white man told her, "Nobody around here wants you here anyway." Early the next morning a large local group that included a farmer, a janitor, and a telephone operator called on her and spoke for the town. "We don't want you to leave. We think you're great," one said.

Professor Cecil Glenn of the University of Colorado in Denver said that many African Americans had gone to live on Native American reservations. He added,

Like the Indians, we were land people, earth people. We
had similar folklore. So there was a strong bond.

During the 1970s and 1980s, black political power, particularly in cities, grew dramatically across America. In 1970, the number of African American elected officials was 1,479, but by 1988, it had soared to 6,793.

Dramatic changes had followed the urban rebellions of the 1960s. American voters increasingly showed a willingness to elect African Americans to city halls in major cities and some smaller ones. By 1973, when Tom Bradley, a former policeman and son of a former Texas sharecropper, was elected mayor of Los Angeles with a 20 percent black population there were 80 black mayors in the United States.

Los Angeles mayor Tom Bradley served his city from 1973 to 1992.

By 1989, 304 African Americans, including 60 women, sat in city halls across the country, and many represented cities in which African Americans were a minority. Black mayors served in Detroit, Michigan; Cleveland, Ohio; Newark, New Jersey; Denver, Colorado; Oakland, California; and New Haven, Connecticut. Others had been mayors in Atlanta, Georgia; Birmingham, Alabama; Baltimore, Maryland; New Orleans, Louisiana; Memphis, Tennessee; Tallahassee, Florida; Charlotte, North Carolina; and Roanoke, Virginia.

African American voting strength in southern states was a tribute to the effectiveness of the federal voting rights law of 1965 and its extensions by Congress. In 1963, Birmingham, Alabama, had been a bastion of segregation and white supremacy. In 1979 Richard Arrington, a son of black sharecroppers, gained 98 percent of the black vote and 12 percent of the white vote to win the mayor's office in a city where two out of three citizens were African Americans. He won one election after another each time with white support.

Black mayors, once elected, often showed staying power, and an ability to win on the basis of their accomplishments rather than their color. Bradley won four additional elections, each by a higher percentage of the voters, and he held his post until he decided in 1992 not to run again. However, he was narrowly defeated in 1982, when he ran for governor of California.

In 1983, Congressman Harold Washington, with the solid support of the black community, gained 51 percent of the total vote to become Chicago's first African American mayor. In some districts he carried 44 percent of the white vote. Washington won reelection in 1987 carrying 20 percent of the citywide white vote and 57 percent of the Hispanic vote.

In the 1983 Philadelphia, Pennsylvania, mayoral race, Wilson Goode, an African American, defeated Italian American mayor

Frank Rizzo by 53.2 percent to 46.8 percent to become the first Black to win this city hall. Voters continued to send Goode to Philadelphia's city hall in one election after another.

Harvey Gantt was the first African American student at Clemson University in South Carolina in 1965. Aided by a scholarship from the Herbert Lehman Fund, he was able to graduate. In 1983 Gantt was elected mayor of Charlotte, North Carolina, a city with a black population of 30 percent. Because of what some called a revolution in attitudes, Gantt carried 41 percent of the vote in predominantly white neighborhoods. In 1990, Gantt tried to unseat conservative Senator Jesse Helms in the Democratic Party primary for senator. But Helms defused the challenge by using TV ads saying Gantt's election would cause whites to lose jobs.

Maine had one of the lowest African American populations in the country in 1988. That year William Burney, 37, was elected mayor of Augusta and became the first Black to capture a Maine city hall.

The year 1989 was one of striking political gains for African American mayoral candidates. New Haven, Connecticut, Kansas City, Kansas, and Seattle, Washington, elected black mayors. And from a white district, Connecticut sent a Republican, Gary Franks, its first African American, to Congress. Franks had held his ground in the 1960s when the Ku Klux Klan burned signs on his lawn and threatened his family.

Congressman Ron Dellums of California, elected in 1970, has served during the terms of six presidents.

The Congressional Black Caucus (CBC), formed in 1970, established an impressive record despite its limited membership. Congressman Parren Mitchell, who served Maryland from 1971 to 1986, was able to secure set-asides for minority businesses. Gus Hawkins, who served California from 1963 to 1990, helped pass an employment bill that included affirmative action provisions. Led by Representative Ron Dellums of California, the CBC was able to win Congressional passage of an antiapartheid act in 1986 that strengthened economic sanctions on South Africa. This set the stage for the release of African National Congress leader Nelson Mandela from 26 years in a South African jail. In 1993, Dellums became chair of the important House Armed Services Committee.

In 1991, Mayor Dinkins welcomed South African freedom-fighter, Nelson Mandela, to America. A dramatic ticker-tape parade for Mandela ended in a city hall ceremony.

The CBC had consistently condemned the congressional funding of every military program while ignoring ghetto neighborhoods and programs for the poor. Each year the CBC's "alternative budget" called for cutting military spending by half and making money available for health care, AIDs research, and schools.

By 1989, African Americans had reached new levels of political power. Ron Brown, who had grown up poor in Harlem, New York, was appointed chairman of the Democratic Party's national committee. In 1993, he was named secretary of commerce by President Bill Clinton.

The most striking victory for urban African Americans, however, was the election of David Dinkins, the great-grandson of a slave, as mayor of New York City. Though the African American population was only 29 percent of the total, Dinkins, a quiet negotiator, drew enough Hispanic and white voters to narrowly defeat a popular Italian American prosecutor, Rudolph Giuliani. Giuliani had the burden of running as a Republican in an overwhelmingly Democratic city.

Secretary of Commerce Ron Brown in 1993.

New Stars in Orbit

For the longest time, the American space program was directed by white men who hired other white men as astronauts. White and black women and black men dreamed of streaking through space in rocket ships but thought they never would.

Guy Bluford was born in 1942 to a mother who was a teacher of special education and a father who was a mechanical engineer. Guy wanted to design planes and be an aerospace engineer. Soon his life's goal was to become an astronaut. Bluford graduated from college and received a master's degree in 1974 and then a doctorate in 1978 from the Air Force Institute of Technology. He next entered the astronaut training program of the National Aeronautics and Space Administration (NASA) and in one year was fully trained for the space shuttle program. Along with him were two other Blacks, Frederick Gregory and Ronald McNair.

Astronaut Mae Carol Jemison

The first space shuttle, *Columbia*, was launched in 1981. The second, *Challenger*, in 1983, took the first white woman, Dr. Sally Ride, on its second flight into space. The next *Challenger* flight included Bluford in a crew of five, making him the first African American in space. He was in charge of the crew's experiments.

Ronald McNair was a mission specialist to a 1984 *Challenger* flight where he worked the cranelike device that lifted astronauts and their equipment into space. He also monitored the TV camera to record maneuvers. McNair, along with teacher Christa McAuliffe, the first private citizen in space, Ellison Onizuka, the first Asian American, and Judith Resnik, the second woman in space, were part of the *Challenger* crew that took off on January 28, 1986. One minute and 13 seconds after it was launched, the *Challenger* exploded into a fireball that killed the entire crew.

Mae Carol Jemison, 35, a doctor and an engineer, became the first African American woman in orbit in 1992. By then, she was one of 16 women in the NASA corps of 92 astronauts. As a child she had longed to travel in space. Jemison said,

It's important not only for a little black girl growing up to know, yeah, you can become an astronaut because there's Mae Jemison. But it's important for older white males who sometimes make decisions on those careers of those little black girls.

Jemison, in the astronaut tradition, carried a few personal items into space, including some West African art objects. She was trying to symbolize that space belongs to all nations, not just those wealthy and industrialized enough to finance space travel. ■

CHAPTER 10

"RUN, JESSE, RUN"

Jesse Jackson was born in Greenville, South Carolina, in 1941 to an unwed teenage mother, Helen Burns. Jesse's father was a married man and next-door neighbor. On the playground, Jesse was teased about not having a father. But his grandmother, Tibby, said it was not where he came from, but where he went that mattered.

As part of the 15 percent black population of Greenville, Jesse attended a segregated school. But the Jacksons were not poor, and Jesse and his brother Charles had good clothing, enough food, and love. Jesse also attended the Longbranch Baptist Church's Sunday school where his mother and stepfather sang in the chorus. In the 9th grade he was elected class president and, because he had maintained a grade average of 80 or over, he became president of the school Honor Society.

As a teenager, Jackson worked at various after-school jobs and at Sterling High School won awards in basketball, football, and baseball. In 1960, he entered college in Greensboro, North Carolina, and became a quarterback on the football team and president of the student body. He soon married Jacqueline Brown.

Jackson took an interest in civil rights activities, and in 1963 he was arrested for participating in a sit-in just as his first child, Santita, was born. The Jacksons joined civil rights demonstrations. That year Jesse Jackson also graduated from college.

In 1965, Jackson enrolled in Chicago's Theological Seminary to become a minister. That March, he organized city students for Dr. Martin Luther King's march from Selma to Montgomery, Alabama.

In 1966, Jackson worked for Dr. King in Chicago as director of Operation Breadbasket, initiated by the Southern Christian Leadership Conference (SCLC). He used the church to mobilize people and for marches on city hall. He recruited whites and Blacks, nuns and priests, and Protestants, Catholics, and Jews.

At age 24, Jackson began Operation Breadbasket to boycott

companies that did not hire black employees. He won his first boy-cott in three days and then pressured the A&P Company to hire African Americans.

In 1968, Jackson worked with Dr. King on the Poor People's March on Washington and was city manager of Resurrection City's tent colony, which included whites, Native Americans, Chicanos, and African Americans. He subsequently forced troublemakers to leave the tent city. He accompanied Dr. King to Memphis, Tennessee, to mobilize striking garbage workers. In April, he was with Dr. King when King was assassinated on the balcony of the Lorraine Motel in Memphis.

In 1971, Jackson formed People United to Serve Humanity (PUSH) to increase jobs for African Americans. By 1974, he had changed the focus of the many young people who were discouraged because they felt that neither their education nor their lives mattered. Jackson sought to drill into youths his own confidence and pride. He shouted,

In October 1990 Jesse Jackson and other members of the Rainbow Coalition protest President Bush's veto of the Civil Rights Act of 1990.

> I am somebody.
> I may be poor,
> but I am somebody!
> I may be poorly educated,
> but I am somebody!
> ...I am God's child.

By 1983, Jackson gained a reputation as the man who asked high school students to remain in school, study hard, and stay away from drugs. Then he announced he would run for president in 1984. He called his movement the Rainbow Coalition and promised it would be made up of people of all colors and backgrounds. Black leaders failed to endorse him, and many denounced him for dividing the Democratic Party. However, his election campaign focused American attention on apartheid, the segregated rule by a white minority in South Africa. He also convinced hundreds of thousands of young Blacks to register and vote.

During his campaign, Jackson made a remark that was insulting to Jewish voters. He apologized many times and told the Democratic National Convention of 1984, "God is not yet finished with me." His speech on TV was one of the high points of the convention:

In May 1988 Jesse Jackson campaigned in Los Angeles, California.

> Our time has come. We must leave the racial battleground and find the economic common ground and moral higher ground. Americans, our time has come.

In 1988, Jackson, urged by crowds to "Run, Jesse, Run," made a second try for the Democratic presidential nomination. This time he had the support of major black leaders. He was the best known of the seven Democratic contenders and the most magnetic speaker. By March 1988, only Al Gore, Michael Dukakis, and Jackson had not been eliminated from the race. Jackson carried Michigan and held 646 delegate votes to Dukakis' 653. Then he lost the New York primary.

Jackson arrived at the Democratic convention in Atlanta with the second-highest number of delegates. He said that his right to run had come through the sacrifice of civil rights martyrs such as Rosa Parks, Fannie Lou Hamer, Viola Liuzzo, Michael Schwerner, and James Chaney. His speech again electrified the convention, but the delegates chose Dukakis and ignored Jackson as his running mate. Republican Party candidate George Bush easily beat the Democratic challengers in the 1988 presidential election.

Jackson continued to appear on picket lines and to lead protest marches. However, he had failed to build his Rainbow Coalition into a functioning organization. Instead, he had stressed his own magnetic personality. When he did not run in 1992, his influence as a leading Democrat diminished. Nevertheless, his speech was still the heart of the 1992 convention, receiving the highest TV ratings. Jackson had lost the power to move his party, but he had inspired millions to register to vote, people who had never bothered to vote before.

Black or African American

On December 19, 1988, a group of African American leaders in Chicago, Illinois, called a press conference to discuss the proper term for their people. The main speaker was Jesse Jackson, the first black man to officially enter a presidential primary race as the potential candidate of a major party.

Jackson said the best term was "African American," and that it was better than "Black" because it rooted people to their original homeland. He felt it was best to give people pride to follow their historical legacy and to establish their linkage to their land of origin.

Few people could have made this announcement without being thought arrogant. But after two dramatic runs for the presidential nomination, Jesse Jackson's leadership in the African American community had been established. His word was listened to far and wide. African American began to catch on. ■

C H A P T E R   11

ETHNIC SURVIVAL IN AMERICA

Seats of authority in business or government once were almost entirely occupied by male white Anglo-Saxon Protestants, or WASPs. Robert Christopher's book, *Crashing the Gates: The De-WASPing of America's Power Elite*, described how people once considered outside the mainstream because they were poor, Catholic, Jewish, or immigrants now helped run the government, key corporations, and important foundations.

In the 1990s names such as Boschwitz, D'Amato, Lautenberg, Inouye, Mikulski, Moynihan, DeConcini, and Cohen could be found in the rolls of the most exclusive club in America, the United States Senate. Lee Iacocca, the son of Italian immigrants, was considered one of the country's most brilliant executives. Henry Kissinger, an immigrant from Germany and a former secretary of state, was considered a brilliant thinker about global problems. Bill Cosby, with a doctorate in education, was a TV superstar, a role model for fathers, and an important American educator. Franklin Thompson, who ran the Ford Foundation, Steven Minter of the Cleveland Foundation, and former diplomat Clifton Wharton, who administered a huge teachers' pension fund, are African Americans. The Council on Foreign Relations was chaired by Greek American Peter Peterson, and its president was Peter Tarnoff, a Jewish American.

Wall Street and Washington, D.C., law firms and corporations once were the exclusive domain of WASPs. By 1990, 15 percent of law partners in major law firms were Catholic, and 41 percent were Jewish.

What had happened to ethnic identity in America and the crises it had created for immigrant families? Much of the pain and strife had dissolved. One reason was the sharp rise in intermarriage between ethnic groups in the 1980s. Among Italian Americans, 77

Mixed-Race Americans

Since many peoples met and married in the New World, there have been an increasing number of people of mixed races. The 1990 census showed that almost ten million citizens, an increase of almost 50 percent in ten years, rejected traditional racial categories as "white," "Black," and "Asian" in favor of "other." More people than ever find themselves angry when asked to fill out a form that under "race" says "check one box only."

At Harvard, so many people have signed application forms by checking more than one box for race, that in 1993 the university announced a multiracial category. In Chicago, Ramona Douglass called multiracial people an unseen minority.

> I live, I breathe, I pay taxes, but
> I'm an "other" on a census form.
> I'm sorry. That's not acceptable.

While only 2 percent of marriages are interracial, births to black-and-white couples have increased more than five times in the years between 1968 and 1988.

By 1991, multiracial student groups had formed at the universities of Michigan, Harvard, Stanford, Kansas State, and two branches of the University of California. Stanford University had a Half Asian People's Association and a black Asian American group called Spectrum. Students found solace and pride in these societies. Karen Downing, founder of the Multiracial Group in Michigan, described its value.

> I don't have to defend myself or hide anything, and I'm not judged on my physical appearance. People acknowledge my multiracial identity.

In 1989, Candice Mills, an African American, and her white husband began to publish *Interrace* for such people. Within a few months *Interrace* had a circulation of more than 8,000 subscribers. ■

Interrace's *editors are Candice Mills and Gabe Grosz, her husband.*

percent of those under 25 had married non-Italians. Among Russian Americans, the figure was 79 percent. Opposition to intermarriage among Jewish Americans in Boston fell from 70 percent in 1965 to 34 percent in 1975. By 1981, a third of Japanese Americans were marrying non-Japanese. Asian-Caucasian marriages increased 70 percent in the ten-year period that ended in 1986. Half of all Native Americans married people who were not Native Americans

America's WASPs had to surrender power to people they had once ridiculed as "hyphenated-Americans." World War II had proven the strength of American diversity by defeating Nazi racism. Veterans who could not have afforded college before World War II were able to attend college under the GI Bill. Their ambitions were raised, and their outlooks about ethnicity and race broadened.

Nevertheless, ethnic identification remained a serious issue for recently arrived immigrants and their children facing the process of Americanization. This is natural during years of adjustment to a new culture as immigrant adults debate traditional values versus American values with their American-educated children. During this age-old argument, parents will propound old ways and learn new ways from their children. Younger immigrants continue to show a remarkable ability to learn English and to adapt to American business methods. Immigrant-owned businesses sprout and thrive in self-contained or supportive immigrant communities. As businesses evolve, ethnic entrepreneurs begin to abandon their ghetto enclaves for the larger society.

Foreign languages have survived in the U.S. only where they are absolutely necessary for business, such as in Chinatowns. They also lasted where the ethnic minority was in close contact with the homeland, as among French Canadian Americans living near the Canadian border, or Mexican Americans who live near or visit

In 1992 these two Indiana women were among many people from all over the U.S. who visited St. Tikon's, America's first Russian Orthodox monastery. It was founded in 1906 in South Canaan, Pennsylvania.

Mexico to see relatives. Nationalist groups, ethnic churches, and their cultural societies have tried to preserve their languages and traditional cultures but with decreasing success. Some have been successful in preserving their religious enclaves, for example, the Amish in Pennsylvania and the Hasidic Jews in Brooklyn, New York.

The experience of coming from foreign stock, however, remained alive in some forms. Children and grandchildren rarely abandoned their parents' religion for another that might seem "more American." The American-born third and fourth generations of immigrants frequently have returned to traditional religious institutions and urged their children to affiliate with them. This return to religion began in the suburbs as a way of making sure the young were introduced to and married people within their religion.

What has also remained alive for ethnic families after language and culture faded is a set of attitudes that express old values about marriage, food, and life in general. Ways of expressing or not expressing emotion and insisting on or rejecting certain foods sometimes unconsciously have reflected ethnic training. Children of immigrant families also have tended to reside in the same locations as their parents — French Canadians in New England; Jewish, Arab, Polish, and Italian Americans in large cities; Scandinavian Americans in rural areas of the Midwest; Japanese and Chinese Americans on the West Coast; Mexican Americans in the Southwest and California. The elderly often have refused to move from childhood neighborhoods, even after multiethnic populations moved into the communities.

Some ethnic neighborhoods remained entrenched in large cities as diluted bastions of former cultural strongholds. Even when an ethnic group moved out of a city neighborhood, it tended to reassemble in identifiable groups in other parts of a city or suburb. This recreated a kind of "made in the USA" version of a culture with strong multiethnic American overtones.

In old neighborhoods, charities established for immigrants and their children welcomed new ethnic groups. Jewish YMHA and Irish and Italian Catholic charities, for example, stayed on to serve a broadly multicultural population.

C H A P T E R   12

COMPETITIVE SPORTS IN AMERICA

American sports have changed radically since 1911 when Francesco Pezzolo became the first Italian American to sign up to play major league baseball with the Chicago White Sox. The Sox manager asked Pezzolo to change his name to Ping Brodie so no one would be offended. Pezzolo played for years as Brodie, including a stint with the New York Yankees as a teammate of Babe Ruth.

By the 1990s, professional teams were recruiting players of all ethnic backgrounds, and race was no longer an issue in sports. Or was it? In 1987, Al Campanis, the general manager of the Los Angeles Dodgers, was asked on television why so few African Americans became baseball executives. He answered, "I truly believe they may not have some of the necessities to be, let's say, a field manager or perhaps a general manager."

The public was shocked at his words. Frank Robinson, Hall of Fame outfielder, had become the first black major league manager in 1970. Finally, said Robinson, someone from baseball's "inner circle had let out what we had known all along."

In 1992, journalist Claire Smith explored the issue of race in sports hiring. She found when it came to choosing people of color as leaders, top executives in professional baseball, football, and basketball "are still measuring their progress in inches." She wrote:

> Those waging the battle — Blacks, Hispanic people, Asians, and whites — are often frustrated with systems and mind-sets that still reflect the words of Campanis more than anyone who has tried to prove him wrong.

In the 5 years after Campanis' remark, Smith found, the 28 major league baseball teams hired 48 managers, and only 6 were minority members. There were 3 black managers in the majors, the

In 1992 a smiling Don Baylor was introduced as the Colorado Rockies baseball team's first manager.

highest to that date, but minority representation as managers, coaches, trainers, scouts, and instructors was only 19 percent. In the front office people of color held only 16 percent of the jobs. Among players, however, 17 percent were African American, and 15 percent were Hispanic Americans.

On the 28 teams of the National Football League in 1992 there were 66 African American coaches. However, in a league where 60 percent of the players are black, there are only two black head coaches, and three black coordinators. In five years, the number of people of color in front office and coach positions rose from 10 percent to 15 percent.

The National Basketball League's 27 teams in 1992 had four black general managers, and five of 79 vice presidents were black. This, said Charles Grantham, director of the Players Association

Art Shell, head coach for the Los Angeles Raiders, watches a 1990 play-off game.

> sends a very clear message to the active black player that if his intention is to continue in this business, there will be a different set of criteria in evaluating him for these positions.

Bill White, the president of baseball's National League and the highest ranking African American in professional sports at that time, was optimistic. He felt public consciousness of the issue had been raised by the Campanis incident, but he added, "the pressure ebbs and flows." Baseball commissioner Fay Vincent offered this summary of progress in baseball:

> Here we are, 17 years after Frank Robinson became the first black manager in the major leagues, and today, in 1992, we have only three minority managers in the major leagues, only three black assistant general managers in the major leagues, and not one black manager in the minor leagues. That is unacceptable.

No one claimed that people of color in professional sports were not qualified nor interested in top positions. In 1991, when many general managers' positions became available in major league baseball, neither Frank Robinson or the two other African American assistant general managers were invited to interviews. Professional sports still needed to be integrated at its top and middle levels.

C H A P T E R   1 3

JUSTICE IN AMERICA

In the decade that ended in 1991, criminal activity by people of all ages had increased by a third. Young people "in all races, social classes, and life-styles," announced the FBI, had an arrest record 27 percent higher than a decade before. The United States had the highest confinement rate in the world. More than one of every 25 American men and one of every 173 women were under the direct control of the criminal justice system.

Substance abuse had also become a national tragedy. In 1992 Columbia University's Center on Addiction and Substance Abuse, headed by former cabinet member Joseph Califano, found that 95 million Americans were addicted to tobacco, alcohol, and/or hallucinatory drugs. This represented a loss to the economy of $300 billion a year and tended to escalate the crime rate. About 80 percent of drug abusers were white Americans, but about 75 percent of those arrested for drug crimes were people of color, mostly young men.

The country spent more money on criminal justice than education. It cost more to keep a person behind bars than it cost to send him or her to the best universities. The United States had a larger percentage of its citizens in jail than South Africa, a country at war with its black population.

Justice, like rain, did not fall equally on all Americans. A commission of 17 prominent citizens including former Secretary of State Cyrus Vance, spent three years examining New York State's legal system. In 1991, it concluded the justice system was unfair to the poor and "infested with racism." The report, said Vance, was "a terrible condemnation of our society." Of the 1,129 state judges the commission found 71 were African American, 19 were Hispanic American, and three were Asian American.

Injustice began with arrests. African American youths between ages 10 and 17 nationwide were arrested for violent crime at five times the rate for whites. Arrests for murder increased 48 percent for white youths and 145 percent for black youths during the 1980s. A New Jersey reporter found that his paper published photographs of black suspects being led away in handcuffs, but "whenever a white person was arrested, they seemed to dig up his graduation picture for the newspaper."

The Accusation

In two dramatic cases, one in Boston, the other in Milwaukee, white men murdered their wives and tried to cover up their crimes by conjuring up black assailants. In Boston, in 1989, Michael Stuart wanted to collect his pregnant wife's $300,000 insurance policy. When he failed to find a hired killer, Stuart drove his wife into a ghetto neighborhood, shot her fatally, wounded himself, and called the police from his car phone to report that a black man had committed the murder.

Police swept through the ghetto and rounded up men who met Stuart's description. On the basis of pictures shown him by the police, Stuart picked his "assailant" from a police lineup. A journalist finally began to uncover Stuart's clever crime. As the net of guilt tightened around him, Stuart took his own life by plunging to his death from a bridge.

In Milwaukee, Wisconsin, in 1992, businessman Jesse Anderson said two black men with knives had assaulted him and his white wife Barbara in a parking lot, stabbed her to death, and left him with three knife wounds.

The police checked Anderson's story. They did not fall for his racist stereotype and did not round up any black men. A jury took nine hours to convict Anderson of the murder. ∎

Police departments throughout the country were overwhelmingly white, sometimes by 95 percent. In New York City in the 1980s, Mayors Edward Koch and David Dinkins selected African Americans as police commissioners. However, the police force remained largely white. Despite minority recruitment efforts, the department was only 13.6 percent Hispanic, 11.5 percent African American, and 1 percent Asian American. About 42 percent of the New York City police lived outside the city and nearly 30 percent far away from their beats, in Queens and Staten Island. Only 3.4 percent lived and served in Manhattan.

People of color, especially in poor or high-crime areas, needed police protection. But they also saw that white police treated ghetto residents as dangerous enemies.

This 1992 police rally at New York's City Hall turned violent when participants hurled racial epithets and tried to push into the building.

Charges of police brutality against ghetto residents were common. In 1992, this issue was highlighted by two incidents. In Brooklyn, 11 white police officers were charged with beating Mrs. Ann Dodds during a domestic dispute at her home. Mrs. Dodds had no record of arrests and had been long admired as the chair of her local school board.

A few months later 10,000 off-duty police demonstrated before New York City Hall to protest a plan by Mayor Dinkins for a civilian review board to review charges of police crimes. After provocative speeches, the police demonstration turned violent. Racial slurs were shouted, some directed at the mayor. Then, thousands of police demonstrators tried to push into city hall, and, when they were repulsed, they blocked the Brooklyn Bridge. Many citizens who had supported the police now said that police misconduct had to be evaluated by more objective citizens of society.

In February 1992, the United States Civil Rights Commission reported that Asian Americans faced widespread racially motivated violence and harassment. "There has been a widespread failure of government at all levels and of the nation's public schools to provide for the needs of immigrant Asian Americans." The commission pointed out that Asian Americans had been considered the "model minority" by a society that admired those educated, affluent, and professional Asians who arrived as immigrants. However, most Asian Americans faced "widespread prejudice, discrimination, and barriers to equal opportunity."

Cultural factors sometime hid crimes against Asian Americans. The commission found that Asian Americans, often failed to report hate crimes because they felt ashamed of being victims or because they did not trust the police.

In 1982, a young Chinese American, Vincent Chin, was asked to a bar by his friends in Detroit to celebrate his coming wedding. Two white autoworkers blamed Chin because they were out of work, called him "a Jap," and beat him to death with a baseball bat. Chin's mother said,

> I don't understand how this could happen in America. My husband fought for this country [in World War II]. We always paid our taxes and worked hard. Before I really loved America, but now this has made me very angry.

Ronald Takaki blamed this kind of racial violence on a school system that failed to teach the values of ethnic diversity and omitted multicultural contributions to America. Dennis Hayashi, director of the Japanese American Citizens League, found the 1992 presidential race had increased "Japan-bashing" by both parties.

> Last year's model minority has become this year's political scapegoat. Just in the past few months we've seen a significant increase in the reports of racial harassment coming into our offices.

Across the country, police departments and courts employed too few interpreters of Asian languages. This resulted in botched criminal investigations and underreported crimes. In Florida, in 1985, a Vietnamese immigrant was on trial for two days for murder — until his attorney and the prison staff realized he was the wrong man.

Mexican Americans long have suffered under a white justice system particularly in the Southwest and California where they are most numerous. However, as more Chicanos are elected and appointed to high office, discrimination has decreased.

In 1992, however, United Farm Workers Union leader Cesar Chavez found the justice system arrayed against his union during a strike. One of his members, Rufino Contreras, was slain. Chavez said the state prosecutors refused to bring Contreras' killers to trial. The state court system also leveled huge fines against his union. He said,

> We work within the system. We follow the rules. And what does it get us? It got Rufino killed....

CHAPTER 14

AMERICAN EDUCATION

The American public education system, say some critics, began to die once it began to lose its white pupils and gain students of color. Between 1968 and 1984, white school enrollment fell by 19 percent. Meanwhile, Hispanic enrollment soared by 80 percent and Asian American enrollment by 41 percent.

Two generations after the Supreme Court outlawed segregation, two-thirds of African American pupils attended schools that had no whites. For example, in Illinois, where African Americans made up 19 percent of the school population, more than 82 percent of African Americans attended segregated schools. In California, where African Americans made up 9 percent, and in Michigan, where they were 20 percent of the school population, 76 percent were in segregated schools.

In his book, *Savage Inequalities*, educator Jonathan Kozol found segregation had returned to schools all over the country. Black educators, he found, no longer discussed how to integrate schools but how to make segregated schools work.

In Los Angeles, the number of white children in school declined from 56 percent to 18 percent in the thirty years ending in 1985. One Oakland elementary school was required by state law to offer instruction in Spanish, Cantonese, Vietnamese, Lao, Khmer, and Tigrinya (an Ethiopian language).

By the 1990s, the arrival of millions of immigrants and refugees, many of them with young children, severely tested education in the United States. Few teachers could speak any language but English. Pupils with "limited English proficiency" numbered 3.5

Classes with students of various ethnic backgrounds, like this one in a middle school in North Carolina, are becoming increasingly representative of many schools across the United States.

million, and half a million more had been placed in special language classes.

Some high schools continued to send graduates on to Yale, Harvard, and Columbia, but others struggled to teach students how to read and write basic English. Few inner-city schools offered courses in computer literacy. Instead many of these ghetto schools had the arduous task of battling a rising dropout rate.

A poor elementary and secondary education for people of color directly affected their success in colleges. In 1988 at the University of California at Berkeley, 71 percent of whites, 67 percent of Asians, 43 percent of Hispanics, and 38 percent of African Americans graduated.

On tests, Asians generally scored highest, whites second highest, Hispanics next, and African Americans last in all income categories. However, family income played a major role in the Scholastic Aptitude Test (SAT) scores. Regardless of race, pupils from families who earned more money did better than those from families who earned less. For example, African American students whose families made $70,000 or more scored 150 points higher than those who made less than $20,000. Both African Americans and Chicanos whose parents earned more money scored higher than Japanese Americans whose parents earned less. However, evidence indicated that those who did well on tests did not necessarily do well in their occupations, social leadership, or accomplishments. Tests had a hidden cultural bias that was easier for some groups to master than others.

In 1988, black enrollment at colleges, particularly private institutions, had fallen since the 1960s to far less than the 13 percent of Blacks in the total population. Harvard and Amherst admissions were only 5.4 percent black, Yale 5.8 percent, and Vassar 7.5 percent, and other colleges had even fewer. Columbia University had 4.2 percent, Smith 3.4 percent, University of Chicago 4 percent. Some public colleges had even lower percentages of black students. The University of California branches at Santa Barbara and Santa Cruz both admitted fewer than 3 percent Blacks. Though Brooklyn College in New York admitted 19.2 percent Blacks, this was lower than the percentage of Blacks in the total population in that borough of New York City. And Queens College in New York admitted only 11 percent in a borough with a black population double that.

Of the 24,721 doctorates awarded by graduate schools in 1991, only 993 went to African Americans, 708 to Hispanic Americans, and 128 to Native Americans. Schools of education turned out few people of color as teachers. Only 8 percent of the nation's teachers were African Americans, and 3 percent were Hispanic Americans. In large cities these percentages of the total population were much larger.

Children of color faced many white teachers who did not expect them to perform. Many pupils were tracked into slower "special education" classes. In Huntington, Long Island, one in ten white students sat in special classes, but for African Americans, the figure was one in three, and for Hispanic Americans, it was one in five.

Children of recent immigrants also found themselves in classes geared for learning at levels below their intelligence. Mrs. Marlene Ben Baruch brought her Israeli-born teenagers to the United States, and the New York State system placed them in special classes. "They're training the foreign students to be either cashiers at the local grocery or short-order cooks," she complained. Many foreign-born mothers and fathers were so overwhelmed by the system's complexity that they did not complain. Victor Jordan, president of the African Caribbean Olive Branch Society said most minority parents "wind up doing as they're told, signing where they're told to sign." Susan Levering, a white attorney who spent two years investigating complaints, found tracking began in Long Island when "black kids got put into the dumb classes."

School guidance counselors often steered students of color away from college and the professions. Guy Bluford, the first African American astronaut, was told by his high school advisor that he was only smart enough for trade school. Brooklyn College student Lisette Nieves kept hearing, "You don't have that thought gene," yet she was the first Puerto Rican to earn a Rhodes Scholarship. Jeffrey Pegram, a Native American who made his high school dean's list three years in a row, was advised by a counselor to join the army or enroll at a two-year college. In 1992 he graduated from the University of Massachusetts. Gonzalo Zeballos, a Chilean American, was admitted to the honors program at Holy Cross College. "You're just the token minority," said one of his best friends. But Zeballos, who graduated with high grades, concluded, "People who want to belittle you or your accomplishments are always going to find a way, and you have to find a way to get beyond that."

The Institute for the Recruitment of Teachers in Andover, Massachusetts, hired a staff comprised of minorities to train promising college students. Training of students took four weeks followed by additional help in graduate school. "We tell them, 'You can do this.' We show them how they can succeed and overcome," explained instructor Noel Anderson. Ray Blakeney, a senior at the University of Dayton in Ohio, born to an African American father and a Korean American mother, was delighted to find "people are out there who really want to help."

In Seattle, Washington, Betty Patu, a Samoan-born high school teacher, developed her own program to keep Samoan, Fijian, Hawaiian, Tahitian, and Tongan students from dropping out of school. Her South Pacific Drop-Out Prevention Program slashed the dropout rate for these groups from over 25 percent to 8.6 percent.

Patu insisted all students arrive in class on time, and she questioned them if they were late. She sometimes drove her car around Seattle searching for them and once barged into a "Crips" gang meeting to bring some students back to class. She even persuaded one gang member to become a recruiter for her class.

Teachers often visited Patu's class to learn her techniques for educating Samoans and other students. "It's amazing, some of these kids are graduating," said a fellow teacher. "All it took was getting them to know we care."

There were signs of hope in American elementary education. The Charles Rice School in South Dallas, Texas, was situated in the middle of a ghetto with a high unemployment rate, a high crime rate, and many crack addicts. The school stressed success. It involved parents and children in key decisions and reached many children with the idea they could become a success if they thought for themselves. "I feel school prepares you to resist peer pressure and prepares you for life. That's what I've learned here," said one student.

Multicultural History

"Without our background, whatever nationality it happens to be, we are nothing," said Mike Krolewski, a Polish American scholar. Yet the nation's schools have traditionally viewed ethnicity as a major obstacle to overcome in order to teach assimilation and Americanization.

Children of color are taught a version of history in which heroes are almost all white. In 1992, Bill Bigelow and other teachers wrote *Rethinking Columbus*. This project was part of a broad effort called "a curriculum of inclusion" to balance the traditional rendition of history that omitted the people of color's role.

Black scholars have tried hard to correct these distortions. In 1841 Dr. James Pennington wrote the first history of African Americans. Scholars W.E.B. Du Bois and Carter G. Woodson wrote dozens of books detailing the truth about people of African descent.

Native Americans had long been taught a European-oriented version of history that glorified the arrival of Columbus on American shores as a discovery. "For Native Americans," said Stephanie Betancourt, a Seneca, "every Columbus Day is like salt in our wounds. These are days of mourning." Evan Haney recalled attending an Indian school with "no books on Indian history, not even in the library."

Mexican Americans also found their heritage had been locked out of the school curriculum. Professor Rudolfo Acuna said, reduced funding had seriously undercut Chicano studies programs in colleges. Most public schools, he said, denied the subject a place in their programs.

The "Curriculum of Inclusion" had made progress among some educators and stirred fervent opposition in others. Critics of multiculturalism claim that it will undermine America's unifying values which they insist stem from English parliamentary influences. New York State Education Commissioner Thomas Sobol appointed a new multicultural task force that in 1989 offered a multicultural curriculum. However, the committee was divided. The majority stated,

> If social studies is to be taught from a global perspective, many of the so-called minorities in America are more accurately described as part of the world's majorities....

On the other hand, Professor Arthur Schlesinger, Jr., of City College, New York, who served on the commission, said the majority position would lead to "ethnic cheerleading" rather than historical truth. ■

This 1992 magazine for teachers offered a multicultural perspective on American history and life.

CHAPTER 15

RACIAL CONFLICT AND COOPERATION

As America increasingly strove to become a more democratic society in the 1990s, the process was not always painless or peaceful. "We are a country of strangers," said black Stanford University professor Anna Deavere Smith in 1992. "And we are having a great deal of difficulty with our differences. Because ultimately, we lack the ability to look at specific human beings."

On August 21, 1991, two black children were hit by a car in the Crown Heights section of Brooklyn, New York. The driver of the car, a Hasidic Jew, was not charged with the subsequent death of one child and injury of the other. Riots broke out in the local black community in response to this decision, and in retaliation an Australian rabbinical student who was walking on the street was stabbed to death. This was followed by three days of rage that tore apart the Crown Heights community shared by Hasidic Jews and Blacks.

In the wake of the violence in Crown Heights, community members in 1992 tried to form interracial alliances. Members of the New York Board of Rabbis and the Haitian Evangelical Clergy

On August 24, 1991, a large group of African Americans in Crown Heights organized a protest march when the driver of a car that killed a black child was not charged with a crime related to the child's death.

Association marched to New York's city hall to protest United States immigration policies that bar most Haitian immigrants and place a ceiling on Jewish immigration from Russia. The two groups condemned the military coup in Haiti that overthrew President Aristide, federal cuts in social programs, and the rise in racism and anti-Semitism. Said Haitian American clergyman Philius Nicolas,

> Wherever there is tension we will stand up....We will stand up against any kind of human rights violation.

Four months later, in the annual West Indian festival in Brooklyn many other groups in addition to West Indians sang and enjoyed the fun on Labor Day. The famous "Calypso King of the World," Slinger Francisco, often called "the Mighty Sparrow," returned from Trinidad that year to celebrate the festival's 25th anniversary. The march moved along Eastern Parkway, which was temporarily renamed Caribbean Parkway through the efforts of Jamaican immigrant Una Clarke, a city council member. The calypso song, "Crown Heights," sought to heal the recent racial scars:

The West Indian Carnival, held in Brooklyn, New York, celebrates the West Indian cultural heritage of some of New York City's residents.

> Preacher man, rabbi or priest
> We must learn to live in peace, live in peace.
> Both of us will suffer loss — history will show
> From slavery to Holocaust, the world will know.
> So we have to live in peace.
> No reason to fight like beasts.
> Live in peace.

Marching arm in arm were New York governor Mario Cuomo, New York City mayor David Dinkins, Reverend Jesse Jackson, Councilwoman Una Clarke, Comptroller Elizabeth Holtzman, and Reverend Al Sharpton. For the first time, the Korean American Association of Brooklyn marched in the parade to show solidarity with West Indian immigrants and other people of color. Wrote reporter James Dao:

> Arguably, there is no more colorful parade in this city known for its parades. There were people dressed as tigers, leopards, African warriors, hawks, magic men, and Inca kings. And every costume seemed an attempt to outdo the next....

Jesse Jackson told the enthusiastic crowd,

> At our worst, we hurt each other. Today, we stand not in hurt, but in hope.

Some people, however, have done their best to undermine harmony and promote racial bigotry and antagonism in America. Since

The Louisiana Governor's Election, 1991

Few would have predicted that an avowed racist might win the governorship of a state in the 1990s. Then, in 1991, David Duke, a former American Nazi and for years a Klan leader, ran for governor of Louisiana as a white supremacist. In 1989, Duke had been elected to the Louisiana legislature by campaigning against affirmative action and minority aid programs.

Former Nazi and Klansman David Duke ran for governor of Louisiana in 1991.

The media said Duke would be lucky to get 10 percent of the vote but treated him as an earnest candidate with a serious message. Leading TV talk-show hosts provided Duke free airtime to express his views. Some even had to agree not to question him about his early racist activity. Money poured into the candidate's treasury from every state. When Duke won 39 percent of the vote for governor, political figures in both parties called it a decisive defeat for racism. Since 55 percent of whites in Louisiana had cast their ballots for David Duke, it was more like a warning bell.

David Duke's defeat was partly engineered by an alliance of African Americans and Jewish Americans. Duke later entered the Republican presidential nomination race but withdrew after a poor early showing. Nevertheless, he has announced his political career is far from over.

The strength of the David Duke campaign was one sign that multicultural America faced an uncertain future. Another sign was the announcement by the Department of Justice that crimes of hate had risen 550 percent in the previous decade. ■

American Skinheads give the Nazi salute after a conference in Idaho that celebrated the 100th birthday of Adolf Hitler in 1989.

1866, the Ku Klux Klan has been on the violent cutting edge of white supremacy in American life. In 1980, Klansman Tom Metzger received 35,000 votes in his unsuccessful bid to gain a congressional nomination from a San Diego district. He claimed his huge vote proved the Klan was representative of white society. By the 1990s, the Klan had become a series of splinter groups that tried to unite with American Nazi fanatics on one hand and conservative political groups on the other.

Neo-Nazi societies have also appeared. Their members wear uniforms with swastikas on occasion and circulate propaganda from the Hitler era that focuses hatred on Jews and people of color.

Recently the fastest growing addition to the white supremacy movement was "skinheads." In 1988, in Portland, Oregon, three young skinheads murdered Mulugeta Seraw, 27, an Ethiopian college student. The three had been in contact with an organization called the White Aryan Resistance, directed by Tom Metzger, and its youth arm, the Aryan Youth Movement, run by his son John.

A Christian identity movement, the Order of Aryan Nations, claimed that the Bible's chosen people are white Anglo-Saxons. It also claimed that Jews are descended from Satan, and people of color are "mud people," a lower human species.

Other white supremacy groups claimed increased memberships. Klanwatch, a society that investigates hate groups, reported that groups espousing anti-Black and anti-Semitic hate rose from 69 in 1989 to 97 the next year. Neo-Nazi, skinhead, and Aryan race clubs rose from 160 to 203 in the same period. By 1990, skinheads had formed groups in 34 states from California to Georgia.

People in the 1990s also had a greater awareness and rejection of violent hate groups. The Anti-Defamation League of B'nai B'rith in New York City had tracked violent hate groups and reported on them to the public and to law enforcement agents for decades. Newer, interracial societies, such as the Center for Democratic Renewal in Atlanta, Georgia, and Klanwatch in Montgomery, Alabama, began to monitor and prosecute hate groups in the 1970s.

In 1986, Morris Dees, Klanwatch's chief attorney, won a $7 million damage suit against the United Klans of America (UKA) on behalf of the mother of Michael Donald, who was lynched by UKA members. The jury award put the UKA out of business.

Dees then won a $12 million suit in 1990 against the White Aryan Resistance for their part in the murder of Ethiopian Mulugeta Seraw in Oregon. Dees said, "The reason we asked for so much, and the reason the jury gave it to us, is the signal it would send to the organized hate business."

By 1992, American Klansmen and Nazis had made contact with neo-Nazi groups in Germany. Assaults on foreigners living in Germany rose from 270 in 1991 to 1,483 the next year. Germany's interior minister Rudolph Seiters reported U.S. Ku Klux Klan leaders had "founded groups in several cities, including Berlin." The leading producer of neo-Nazi materials for Germany was a publishing firm in Lincoln, Nebraska.

The media has often considered Nazi, Klan, and other racists hot news. Media critic Michael Parenti claimed the media publicized racists' words and ignored their violence:

> The press regularly fails to report the Klan's worst
> features, saying almost nothing about its history of
> violence, arson, terrorism, murder, and lynching. Some of
> that history is not far past. In the last 15 years, at least nine
> persons have died at the hands of Klan members, while
> scores have been harassed, intimidated, or injured.

Racism in America has proven to be an ongoing problem that each generation has to deal with.

CHAPTER 16

LOS ANGELES, 1992

Rodney King had an arrest record and a bad reputation when Los Angeles police stopped him on March 3, 1992, for driving while drunk and speeding. King was pulled from his car and fell to the ground. As more than a dozen witnesses looked on, four officers struck King's head and body 56 times with their nightsticks while King tried to crawl away.

Ghetto inhabitants have often insisted that the police act brutally toward nonwhite suspects, but few whites have believed them. This time a white citizen recorded the event with his video camera. The videotaped police beating of King appeared first in Los Angeles, then all over the country and the world.

Four Los Angeles police officers were charged in the King beating. Pretrial publicity led a judge to reassign the case to a nearby white suburb in Simi Valley. On April 29, 1992, a jury of 10 whites, an Hispanic, and an Asian American acquitted the four officers of all major charges.

"The verdict removed the pretense of justice," said Medria Williams an African American psychologist in Los Angeles.

So many times we've been told,"Just be patient, the
system will work," that what we experience isn't real. This
lifted the veil from that and exposed it.

Factory owner Norwood Clark said the verdict was enough to make him give up on whites.

Here I am doing the right thing, running a business,
obeying the law. I believe in the Constitution. . . .White
people won't ever look at us eye-to-eye as equals.

Within hours of the jury verdict, the ghetto of South Los Angeles exploded in violence. Fires gutted buildings, and businesses and cars were overturned and set afire. Some whites driving

Reverend Murray's Lesson

The night the Los Angeles riot began, Reverend Cecil Murray of the First African Methodist Episcopal Church and some parishoners stood between 25 police officers and 150 local residents armed with rocks. Reverend Murray tried to heal the wounds of his city:

You can't ask preachers of peace to spend all their time with the victims saying, "Be cool and accept the status quo; you don't give in to your anger." You have no respect among people if you spend your time talking to black faces when you ought to be talking to white faces. Black people are not black people's problems. White people are black people's problems. ■

through the area were pulled from their cars. Violence spread when police were withdrawn from, rather than sent into, the riot area. In the middle of the uprising Rodney King appeared on TV to ask for peace and pleaded for the rioters to go home. "The violence is wrong," he said. Few listened.

Firebombing spread from South Los Angeles to middle-class white neighborhoods. Korean American merchants were often tar-

A local Korean American merchant surveys his burned-out store during the Los Angeles riots of 1992.

A National Guard soldier stands watch outside a toy store after capturing looters inside during the Los Angeles riots.

geted, and over 1,800 Korean American businesses worth $300 million were destroyed or vandalized. Businesses owned by African Americans and others also went up in flames. When the upheaval was over, 51 people had died, 18,000 had been arrested, and there was $850 million in damages. National Guard troops finally restored order. The United States had suffered its largest urban riot. Some called it a rebellion.

Marlin Fitzwater, spokesperson for President George Bush, blamed the violence on President Johnson's "Great Society" programs in the 1960s. Asked which programs, he said "I don't have a list with me." Vice President Dan Quayle blamed the riot on lawbreakers and the breakdown of family values. He praised the police.

People of color saw it differently. "If the Kurds stood up to Hussein, the U.S. would applaud them," said Shaka Ali, owner of an art gallery near the riot zone. "But somehow it's not legitimate for us to rise up no matter how bad things get."

Many whites condemned the violence as unjustified, especially the assault (also videotaped) on an innocent white truck driver, Reginald Denny, who happened to drive into the riot area. Denny's assailants were arrested. Professor Adolph Reed of Northwestern University offered this analysis:

> The people who beat the truck driver was a mob. The people who beat Rodney King were public officials. In principle, if the truck driver had 25 cents and somehow could have gotten to a pay phone, he could have called 911 and gotten help. If Rodney King had a bag full of

quarters in his pocket, he couldn't call 911 because it was the cops beating him up.

President Bush arrived to tour the riot area. In a black church nearby he prayed to God to help solve urban unrest. For people of color, the sight of a president on his knees praying for heavenly guidance indicated not religious faith but a helpless inability to understand or solve basic ghetto problems.

In 1992 Maxine Waters and Jesse Jackson call on the United States Justice Department to investigate four Los Angeles police who beat Rodney King.

Congresswoman Maxine Waters, who represented the Los Angeles district in Congress, called it a predictable "insurrection" against ghetto conditions. The *Los Angeles Times* reported that the income of black teenagers between 1973 and 1986 had fallen by 44 percent, the rate for Hispanic Americans by 35 percent. "People of color were protesting not just the Rodney King verdict but the conditions of poverty, violence, and frequent police harassment which are at the center of ghetto life," said Professor Manning Marable of the University of Colorado.

Other people of color saw the Los Angeles violence as a rebellion against misplaced American priorities. Benjamin Hooks of the NAACP said, "We must say to President Bush: Let us be as concerned about Sacramento as we are about Saudi Arabia, as concerned about Los Angeles as we are about Lebanon."

James Johnson, director of the Center for the Study of Urban Poverty at the University of California in Los Angeles, saw "the seeds of the rebellion" in the loss of 200,000 jobs in the riot area during the last 11 years. He said,

> These were high-paying, highly unionized jobs in manufacturing, jobs that were the lifeblood of the community in South Central Los Angeles, providing stable employment and livable wages that allowed people to maintain stable families.

Massive unemployment and schools with a 60 percent to 80 percent dropout rate, said Johnson, provided young men with neither work nor school. The arrival of many young Hispanic Americans searching for work pitted one ethnic group against another. Korean Americans also demanded their share of jobs in the declining economy. These factors became, said Johnson, the "lethal combination," and the King verdict became the spark.

Scholar Cornel West saw the violence as neither a class rebellion nor a race riot, but "a monumental... multiracial, trans-class and largely male display of justified social rage." He pointed out that only 36 percent of the arrested were African Americans, and more than a third of the arrested had full-time jobs. Hundreds of Hispanic and Asian Americans participated in the rebellion.

West said whites immediately discussed the violence in terms of "we and them" rather than approaching it as a problem for all Americans to solve. He said, "If we go down, we go down together" and offered this advice:

> To engage in a serious discussion of race in America, we
> must begin not with the problems of black people but
> with the flaws of American society — flaws rooted in
> historic inequalities and long-standing cultural
> stereotypes. . . .As long as black people are viewed as
> "them," the burden falls on blacks to do all the "cultural"
> and "moral" work necessary for healthy race relations.
> The implication is that only certain Americans can define
> what it means to be American — and the rest must simply
> "fit in."

When Disneyland job recruiters arrived in South Los Angeles two weeks after the riots, they found 600 well-dressed young black men and women at the African Methodist Episcopal Church ready to sign up for jobs. "They were wonderful kids, outstanding kids," said Greg Albrecht, a Disneyland spokesperson. "We didn't know they were there."

One was Olivia Miles, 18, the youngest of 7 children, who graduated from Washington Preparatory High School and was accepted at Grambling State University in Louisiana. All of her brothers and sisters had graduated from high school and had jobs. "My mama tells me, 'Be the best of everything; be proud, be black, be beautiful,'" said Miles, who wants to become a lawyer.

The high school Miles attends has a 70 percent African American and a 30 percent Hispanic American population. "I have a lot of Olivias," said its principal, Marguerite La Motte. That June, Washington's senior class sent 249 students from its graduating class to two- or four-year colleges.

Olivia Miles did not attend her prom — it was canceled by the riots. Her father told her to "just stay in the house" during the uprising, and she did. But the King verdict made her ask her father, "Why am I working so hard? Why have you been telling me that I can achieve?" He urged her to keep trying. She was delighted when she got the Disneyland job at $5.25 an hour.

However, few black residents were hired to clean up the property damage. As white laborers built a new shopping center in the area, Jack Bellamy of the Black Carpenters Association shouted at them,

> You white guys won't give us black people a chance. You aren't fair. You don't know nothing about fair. Black men can do this work, too. They need to do this work to give their children a better future. Is your child better than mine?

The Loss of a Tradition

One of the ruined stores in South Los Angeles was the Aquarian Bookshop with its 5,000 volumes. Perhaps the longest-operating black-owned bookstore in America, it had opened in 1941. The Aquarian Bookshop was also a cultural hub since its founder and owner Dr. Alfred Ligon, 86, encouraged and invited scores of African American writers such as Alex Haley, Alice Walker, and Earl Ofari Hutchinson for book signings. Said Hutchinson,

He has nurtured generations of black writers, artists, scholars, and community activists. That was his mission in life. When I would go in there — and others tell the same story — he would always point out books to us, take a personal interest in our development.

Hutchinson led a fund-raising effort to help Ligon reopen his store, and many publishers offered help by donating books. Said writer Wanda Coleman, "Our tradition was burned down." She felt it was "really important to the health of the black community here that it be rebuilt." ∎

C H A P T E R   17

AMERICAN WOMEN AT THE CROSSROADS

In the 1992 presidential campaign, the Republican Party called itself the defender of "family values." Conservative leaders of the party defined these values to mean opposition to abortion, unwed motherhood, and homosexuals. At the party convention Marilyn Quayle, the vice president's wife, scoffed at mothers who chose careers over rearing children and serving their husbands. Mrs. Quayle has a law degree but abandoned legal work for a while to be a wife and mother. Other wives and mothers claimed a right to choose their own career or job without being accused of degrading family values.

American women generally defined their "family values" in far wider and more complex terms. Millions of wives wanted to remain at home. But others, who loved their children and husbands no less, wanted or needed to work.

Financial conditions drove many mothers to seek jobs. In 1990, 58 percent of mothers with children under age six were part of the labor force, and most worked full time. In 1960 only 20 percent of mothers held jobs.

Not all who worked were driven by necessity. Many loved their jobs, preferring to work rather than staying home, even though most preferred part-time jobs. "I think you can work and be a good mother," said Mrs. Nancy Cassidy of Easton, Pennsylvania.

About 29 percent of families were headed by a single parent, up from 12.9 percent in 1960. Almost 60 percent of

With more women at work, day-care centers have become a pressing issue for many families in the 1990s. This day-care center is in northern California.

single mothers had joined the labor force of the 1990s. Many affluent wives also chose to take jobs in their search for self-fulfillment.

Many mothers had mixed feelings about leaving for work when that meant placing their children in the hands of child-care workers who might not always be the best qualified. Some mothers who sought self-realization in work in the 1990s found the business recession had turned their jobs into necessities. Other mothers found their work gave them a new sense of independence and identity, and a temporary escape from housework and children. They saw work enabling them to become better and more devoted parents. "Being a good mother depends on what type of person you are and what you instill [in your children]," said Mrs. Elesha Lindsay, who worked in a North Carolina hospital.

Women have increasingly been entering fields traditionally dominated by men. In 1991, 87,000 women had jobs in the construction business, while 164,000 women held jobs as mechanics.

Since World War II, women in the labor force had tried hard to narrow the income gap with men and to gain nontraditional jobs. The gap narrowed in the ten years ending in 1989 as women's median wages increased by 78 percent. However, men were six times as likely as women to earn $75,000 or more. Women gained in many work areas. Four out of five new businesses were started by women, and women ran a third of the 20 million small businesses in the United States. Each decade there were more women plumbers, lawyers, doctors, carpenters, and electricians. American mothers also had more children. The number of babies born in the United States has risen each year since 1977 to reach 4.2 million in 1990, up a third since 1976. More than half of the working women who have babies return to work within a year of giving birth.

The number of households headed by single parents increased to over seven million in the 1980s, and nine out of ten were headed by women. Poverty was often prevalent in these households. In Connecticut, in 1980, where 8 percent of the people lived below the federal poverty line, more than 60 percent of these were in female-headed households. In New Jersey 9 percent of the population lived in poverty, but more than 61 percent of female households were below the poverty line. About 25 percent fewer people in these two states lived in poverty in 1990, but the percentage for poor female-headed households declined by less than 25 percent. Poverty therefore was a condition that affected American women and children disproportionately.

Women in the Gulf War

One out of every nine members of the U.S. armed forces in 1992 was a woman. Major Rhonda Cornum was a wife and mother and a U.S. Army flight surgeon with a doctorate in biochemistry. Trained as a paratrooper and helicopter pilot, she was sent to fight in the Persian Gulf. After capturing Iraqi prisoners of war, she wrote her mother that this was one of the most exciting things she had done.

Iraqis shot down Cornum's helicopter killing five crew members. When captured, she had suffered two broken arms, an injured knee, and a bullet wound in her shoulder. She was spared the beatings given captured men but was sexually violated by her guards.

Upon her release, Cornum testified to Congress about her ordeal. She remained on active duty, though her left arm was held together by a steel rod, her little finger held by a screw, and her right knee by a ligament graft. She wrote of her wartime experience in *She Went to War: The Rhonda Cornum Story.* ∎

On political and social issues, American women were hardly a monolithic force. Many, especially young women in urban and suburban areas, voiced agreement with the National Organization for Women (NOW). They sought equality on the job and everywhere else in American life.

But many others disagreed strongly with NOW and affirmed the "family values" defined by the Republican Party. Phyllis Schlafly became the spokesperson for those who she said preferred the traditional values. She assailed NOW and those women she said sought to undermine men. Schlafly felt the independent professional woman offered young people the wrong role model. However, her undeniable capabilities in leadership and oratorical strengths seemed to mirror her targets.

Women clearly were determined to gain a larger share of political power. They had held only 3.5 percent of all state offices in 1969, but by 1983, this had increased to 13 percent.

Phyllis Schlafly in 1988 led a "baby buggy brigade" in Washington, D.C., to protest a federal day-care bill.

Vice presidential candidate Geraldine Ferraro answers reporters' questions during the 1984 campaign.

In 1984, the possibility of a woman in the White House took a dramatic step forward with the selection of Geraldine Ferraro as the Democratic Party's vice presidential candidate. Ferraro was a Queens, New York, congresswoman of Italian American descent. In a televised debate Ferraro held her own against Vice President George Bush on a variety of issues and chided Bush for his patronizing attitude toward her as a woman. Millions of viewers were thrilled with Ferraro's debating abilities and political knowledge.

In 1987, Congresswoman Pat Schroeder announced she was considering a run for the presidency. Few questioned her competence as a legislator or her knowledge of government. But the media repeatedly treated her as a "woman candidate." Due to a lack of popular support, she finally withdrew from the race.

The conservative Reagan and Bush years reversed some feminist gains and muffled others. But the conservative trend against feminism had been under way since the late 1970s. The Equal Rights Amendment (ERA) to the Constitution was wrecked by a strong counteroffensive launched by Mrs. Schlafly. In 1975, New Jersey and New York, states that originally had passed ERA, reversed their vote and killed ERA's chances for passage.

When the Supreme Court ruled that abortion was legal, Mrs. Schlafly mobilized her forces to reverse the ruling. Presidents Reagan and Bush chose Supreme Court justices who they felt opposed the right to abortion. The two Republican presidents saw that their party adopted a social agenda proposed by Schlafly and religious fundamentalists.

The nomination of Judge Clarence Thomas to the Supreme Court by President Bush in 1991 brought about a feminist revival. In an FBI report Professor Anita Hill had charged that, while Thomas was her boss in two federal agencies, he had repeatedly sexually harassed her.

Women in Politics

Born in 1936 in Baltimore, Maryland, to Polish immigrants, Barbara Mikulski was elected and served for eight years on the Baltimore City Council and ten years in the House of Representatives. She showed remarkable political skills as she traveled around the state and repeatedly defeated various Republican candidates in elections. In 1970, Mikulski sounded a new note of pride for ethnic Americans and hope for America.

In 1986, when she was elected to the United States Senate from Maryland, Mikulski became the first woman Democrat elected as a senator in her own right. Calling herself "an idealist and a pragmatist," Mikulski was an ardent feminist and a spokesperson for working-class European Americans. She supported civil rights legislation and an alliance of the poor across racial lines.

Senator Mikulski favored low-cost housing, environmental protection, space probes, and a national long-term health care program. In 1987 *Ms.* magazine named her "Woman of the Year."

In 1992, on the first night of the Democratic National Convention, Senator Mikulski enthusiastically introduced ten Democratic women candidates for the U.S. Senate. "They will be joining me," she told a nationwide television audience. She won reelection with 71 percent of the vote and was joined by four other women Democrats in the Senate in 1993.

Pat Schroeder, born in 1940 in Oregon, graduated from Harvard Law School in 1964, married, and had two children. Then in 1972, without holding any office before, she was elected to the House of Representatives where she eventually became the woman who had served longest in Congress.

Schroeder fought sex discrimination, called for deep cuts in the military budget, opposed the Gulf War, and spoke for the rights of children. She was always ready to champion unpopular causes and take the consequences.

Schroeder often teamed up with Ron Dellums of California, an African American congressman, to challenge Presidents Reagan and Bush. Her barbed wit sometimes offended her political allies.

Schroeder had a deep interest in the preservation of the family and had written a book, *Champion of the Great American Family*. She had sponsored a family leave bill allowing workers to be absent without pay to take care of ill family members. She had long championed a woman's right to choose abortion and had urged the air force to allow women to volunteer for combat.

In 1988, Schroeder decided to enter the Democratic Party's presidential primary. She withdrew after failing to attract enough campaign funds and supporters. In her own district, however, she had consistently beaten each challenger, including four Republican women in the last four elections. ■

Congresswoman Pat Schroeder in 1992.

The Right to Choose

In 1991, Faye Wattleton, the African American president of Planned Parenthood, received the Tom Paine Award for defending human rights from the National Emergency Civil Liberties Committee. Wattleton talked about Margaret Sanger and today's women in her acceptance speech.

Seventy-five years ago, Margaret Sanger opened a storefront clinic in Brooklyn, New York, to give birth control information to poor women in desperate need. The clinic stayed open for ten days before the police closed it down, but they were ten days that shook the world. Today, there's an entire generation of young women who have never known a time when they were not free to make and carry out their own decisions about their bodies and their lives....

Faye Wattleton, president of Planned Parenthood.

Women are learning a bitter lesson. The battle of our lives is not about abortion! The battle of our lives is not about fetuses! The battle of our lives is about whether we will control our lives! It's about whether our role in society will remain a secondary one, and whether our bodies will be controlled by the government in order to keep us in check!

...Our issues are not trivial because our lives are not trivial. Reproductive freedom is not a single issue — it's a fundamental issue — as fundamental as freedom of speech, freedom of the press, freedom of religion, freedom to assemble here today! ■

Until that moment, sexual harassment was a topic rarely mentioned by the media or discussed by men. But in October 1991, seven Democratic congresswomen dramatically marched to the United States Senate and knocked on the door of the regular Democratic Caucus to demand that Hill's charges be heard at an open hearing of the Judiciary Committee. The caucus, composed of men except for Maryland's Senator Barbara Mikulski (who agreed with the seven congresswomen), denied the women entrance. Finally, Senate Majority Leader George Mitchell agreed to meet with the irate congresswomen. The seven then went on to lobby other senators about the Thomas nomination. The offices of Barbara Mikulski and Republican Nancy Kassebaum, the only other woman senator,

With her testimony, Professor Anita Hill made the all-male Senate Judiciary Committee and all Americans conscious of the crime of sexual harassment.

were flooded with phone calls. Women demanded the vote on Thomas be delayed until Hill was heard.

Responding to mounting pressure, the Senate Judiciary Committee held televised hearings on Thomas' nomination. A nationwide television audience listened to detailed sexual charges by Hill and strong refutations by Thomas. Many were incensed at the grilling of Hill by the all-male judiciary committee.

Thomas was finally confirmed. But more women than ever before determined they would no longer be underrepresented in Congress or the Senate. It had been impossible, they said, for Hill to achieve justice before an all-male committee. In 1992, a record number of women ran for the United States Senate.

Feminists of Color

Women of color slowly began to mount their own campaigns against sexism. Some admitted they had learned a lot about sexism from organizations such as NOW. Some claimed, however, that white women's groups greeted them with "outright discrimination" or found it hard to embrace women less affluent and less educated and with vastly different problems.

Women of color began their own brand of feminism to challenge "the multiple sources of oppression" such as race, sex, and lack of opportunity. Chicano leader Consuelo Nieto said that women "must demand that dignity and respect within the women's rights movement which allows her to practice feminism within the context of her own culture." Scholar Ngan-Ling Chow said Asian American feminists were wrongly criticized for "weakening the male ego" and "undermining ethnic unity for Asian Americans as a whole."

By the 1980s, a consensus began to grow among women of color. In 1982, at a University of California feminist discussion, Chicano women defined their role:

> We challenge the notion that there is no room for a Chicana movement within our own community. We, as women of color, have a unique set of concerns that are separate from white women and from men of color.

Throughout the decade, African, Asian, Puerto Rican, and Mexican American women examined what they called "the intersection of race, class, and gender" and its implications. Books and articles appeared on the subject by many women, including African Americans Andrea Lord and Angela Davis, Chicanos Patricia Zavilla, Denise Segura, and Vicki Ruiz, and Asian Americans Esther Chow, Katheryn Fong, and Germaine Wong. ∎

CHAPTER 18

"THE YEAR OF THE WOMAN"

1992 was termed "the Year of the Woman" because so many women ran for and were elected to high office. Women, at 52 percent of the population, were credited with electing Arkansas governor Bill Clinton to the White House. The election also saw women win 20 percent of all state legislative posts. In 1992, 11 women ran for the U.S. Senate, and six were elected to the 100-seat body that previously had only two women senators. Barbara Boxer and Dianne Feinstein were elected to represent California in the Senate. This was the first time both senators from a state were women.

Illinois sent the first African American woman, Carol Braun, to the Senate after she had defeated incumbent Senator Alan Dixon in the primary. In the state of Washington, Patty Murray, who called herself "just a mom in tennis shoes," was elected to the Senate. In Pennsylvania, a political unknown, Lynn Yaekel, almost defeated

Carol Braun, candidate for the U.S. Senate, addresses the 1992 Democratic National Convention in New York City.

Emily's List

In 1988, Ellen R. Malcolm decided that someone had to do something to change the underrepresentation of women in the Senate and House. She put up some of her own money and asked other women for cash contributions to finance Democratic women candidates most likely to succeed. Malcolm's plan took its name from the initials of "Early Money Is Like Yeast" and was called "Emily's List." The idea behind Emily's List was to help elect selected women candidates by providing early funding for their primary and election campaigns. In 1992, Emily's List supported 30 women Democratic candidates, 11 in California alone. ■

Senator Arlen Specter, the chief interrogator of Anita Hill during the Senate hearings on Supreme Court nominee Clarence Thomas.

Moreover, 106 women won primary elections in order to run for the 388 seats up for election in the House of Representatives. (In 1990 only 70 won primaries.) The 47 winning candidates increased the number of women in the House by 15 from the previous 28.

In California's primaries 127 women had run for open seats in the legislature — 35 in the House of Representatives and two for the Senate. In Florida more than a dozen women ran for Congress.

Senators Braun and Murray were typical of the new, assertive American woman who took time off from raising a family to run for high office. In her home Murray raised two teenagers and cared for her aging parents. A former federal prosecutor and state representative, Braun raised her 14-year-old son by herself. She barnstormed her state to pick up support from both Democrats and Republicans who wanted to see more women in the Senate. A reporter wrote:

> To many, Ms. Braun is a defiant Everywoman whose image is only enhanced by revelations that she survived beatings by her policeman father, a divorce, and the death of a brother from drugs and alcohol.

Women were not the only victors in the elections. In 1982 when the Voting Rights Act had come up for renewal, Congress wanted to insure that minorities received greater federal representation. It passed a law that virtually required states where possible to create districts with African American and Hispanic voting majorities. By

1992, state legislatures had shaped many new minority districts. The number of districts with a black voting majority rose from 17 to 32 and with a Hispanic majority from 10 to 19. However, even with these districts the African American 12.1 percent only had voting majorities in 7.4 percent of the congressional districts, and the Hispanic 9 percent of the population had a voting majority in only 4.4 percent of congressional districts. In 1992, Congress had 26 African American and 14 Hispanic members. In 1993, House membership included 39 African Americans and 19 Hispanic Americans.

John Lewis, a leading fighter for the right to vote who had served in Congress from Georgia since 1987, said,

> The goal of the struggle for the right to vote was to create an interracial democracy in America. It was not to create separate enclaves or townships. The Voting Rights Act should lead to a climate in which people of color will have an opportunity to represent not only African Americans but also Hispanic Americans and all Americans.

In 1993 President Bill Clinton gave his State of the Union address to the joint session of Congress. Among the congresspersons in attendance were 6 women senators and 47 women representatives.

CHAPTER 19

INTO THE 21ST CENTURY

Americans approached the 21st century with increased hope about the future. With a new president, Bill Clinton, and a new party in the White House, citizens talked of change and progress. There was the usual gap between the promise and reality of America. Young women in 1990 earned 80 cents for every dollar men earned, but this was up from 69 cents a decade earlier. People of color earned even less and had made even fewer gains then white males.

Progress sometimes seemed disastrously slow in a highly technical world. The dropout rate for U.S. schools was 27 percent compared to 10 percent for Japan. America was 13th out of 20 modern industrialized nations in yearly expenditures for students. Discrimination in the United States was still accepted. A survey in 1992 showed that while 9 percent of middle-class whites were rejected for home loans, for middle-class African Americans, the figure was 23 percent.

The 47 largest urban school sytems with 13 percent of the nation's total school enrollment had 32 percent of all Latinos, 37 percent of all African Americans, and only 5 percent of whites. These districts had 25 percent of the children who lived in poverty and spent on an average only $5,200 a year per pupil. Suburban schools had largely white enrollments and spent $6,200 per year per pupil.

Immigrants continued to make their contributions to the United States despite the enormous problems they faced adjusting to a new land. However, their hope has traditionally recharged American dreams, and their energy has powered progress.

But the greatest encouragement came from recent strides in democratizing the political process. Taking politics seriously, more people of color and women than ever before sat in Congress, in state legislatures, as federal, state, and local judges, and as city mayors. A Native American, an Hispanic American, and six women sat in the United States Senate. Jay Kim, a Republican from southern

California, was the first Korean American elected to Congress.

In 1992, Atlanta, Georgia, elected a black female sheriff Jackie Barrett, who had a master's degree in sociology and 16 years in law enforcement. "You don't set out to make history, it just happens," she said. "You know you will be under a microscope, and that just makes you work that much harder." Sheriff Barrett's words reveal that the pioneer spirit and grit of the working men and women that built the United States is still alive.

The New President's Cabinet

Not until President Franklin D. Roosevelt in 1933 did a woman sit in a presidential cabinet, and not until President Lyndon Johnson in 1964 was a man of color appointed to one. Two decades after Johnson, presidential cabinets did not include more than one woman and one African American and sometimes not even one of each. President Bush's cabinet included 11 white men, 3 women, an Hispanic, and an African American.

In 1992, President Bill Clinton's cabinet choices, he said, "come from all across America" — 7 white men, 3 women, 4 African Americans (including a woman), and 2 Hispanic Americans. Clinton dramatically selected women and people of color for cabinet positions they had been denied before. A woman became secretary of health and human services (Donna Shalala), secretary of energy (Hazel O'Leary), and attorney general (Janet Reno). An African American (Ron Brown) was appointed secretary of commerce, another (Michael Espy) secretary of agriculture, and still another (Jesse Brown) secretary of veterans affairs. One Mexican American, Henry Cisneros, became secretary of housing and urban development, and another, Mexican American, Federico Pena, became secretary of transportation. Professor Madeleine Albright, born in Prague, Czechoslovakia, was chosen to be the U.S. ambassador to the United Nations, a position Clinton promised to raise to cabinet level. Clinton's cabinet, *The New York Times* wrote, "looks like America." ■

President Clinton addresses members of his staff at the White House.

FURTHER READING

Carson, Clayborne, et al. ed. *The Eyes on the Prize Civil Rights Reader: Documents, Speeches, and Firsthand Accounts from the Black Freedom Struggle, 1954-1990*. New York: Penguin, 1991.

Daniels, Roger. *Coming to America: A History of Immigration and Ethnicity in American Life*. New York: HarperCollins, 1990.

Debo, Angie. *A History of the Indians of the United States*, rev. ed. Norman, OK: University of Oklahoma Press, 1984.

The Ethnic Chronology Series. Dobbs Ferry, NY: Oceana Publications, 1972-1990.

Evans, Sara M. *Born for Liberty: A History of Women in America*. New York: Free Press, 1989.

Franklin, John Hope. *From Slavery to Freedom: A History of Negro Americans*, rev. ed. New York: Alfred A. Knopf, 1988.

The *In America* Series. Minneapolis, MN: Lerner Publications, 1971-1990.

Millstein, Beth and Bodin, Jeanne, eds. *We, the American Women: A Documentary History*. New York: Ozer Publishing, 1983.

Seller, Maxine S. *To Seek America: A History of Ethnic Life in the United States*. New York: Ozer Publishing, 1983.

————, ed. *Immigrant Women*. Philadelphia: Temple University Press, 1981.

Takaki, Ronald T. *Strangers from a Different Shore: A History of Asian Americans*. New York: Penguin Books, 1990.

Thernstrom, Stephan, ed. *Harvard Encyclopedia of American Ethnic Groups*. Cambridge, MA: Belknap Press, 1980.

INDEX

Abortion, 84, 86
African Americans, 6, 8, 43–50, 80
AIDS, 44
Alcoholism, 41–42
American Museum of the Moving Image, 12
Anderson, Jesse, 62
Anti-Defamation League of B'nai B'rith, 74
Apartheid, 53
Aquarian Bookshop, 80
Aristide, Father Jean-Bertrand, 23
Arrests, 61–62, 77
Arrington, Richard, 47
Asian Americans, 6, 8, 27–32, 33–38, 63
Asian Indian, 27, 30, 32

Barikhnovskaya, Yelena, 25
Barrett, Jackie, 93
Baseball, 59–60
Baylor, Don, 59
Belilovsky, Anatoly, 25–26
Black film directors, 44
Black vs. African American, 54
Bluford, Guy, 50, 67
Boat people, 22, 23, 35
Boston, 9
Boxer, Barbara, 89
Boycotts, 17, 51–52
Bradley, Tom, 46–47
Braun, Carol, 89, 90
Breadun, Deaglan de, 26
Brodie, Ping, 59
Brown, Ron, 49
Buried Mirror, The (Fuentes), 15
Bush, George, 53, 78, 84, 85

Cambodians, 37
Campanis, Al, 59
Campbell, Ben Nighthorse, 42
Casinos, 41
Castano, Monica, 9
Census (1990), 6, 9, 27, 30, 39
"Chain-reaction" immigration, 33
Challenger, 50
Champion of the Great American Family (Schroeder), 85
Chaplin, Charlie, 12
Chavez, Cesar, 17, 64
Children, 38, 39, 57
    and poverty, 8, 83
    in school, 12–13, 67–68
Chin, Vincent, 64
Chinatown, 28–29, 31, 34
Chinese Americans, 28–29, 33–34
Cisneros, Henry, 15
Citizenship, 11–12
Civil Rights Commission report, 31
Clinton, Bill, 15, 92, 93
Coffee, Wallace, 40
College, 27–28, 31, 57, 66

Communities Organized for Public Service (COPS), 15
Congressional Black Caucus (CBC), 48–49
Copage, Eric, 45
Cornum, Major Rhonda, 83
Crashing the Gates: The De-WASPing of America's Power Elite (Christopher), 55
Cuban Americans, 21–23
"Curriculum of Inclusion", 69

Day-care centers, 81
Dellums, Ron, 48–49, 85
Denny, Reginald, 77
Dinkins, David, 16, 18, 49, 63
Dodds, Ann, 63
Dominican Republic, 20, 21
Dropout rate, 68, 78, 92
Drugs, 61
Duke, David, 72

East Indians, 29–30, 38
Economist, The, 35
Edin, Kathryn, 44
Education, 11, 12–13, 65–69
    of Asian Americans, 27–28, 31
    of Laotians, 36
Emily's List, 90
English as a Second Language, 11, 28
English language, 17, 28, 29, 38, 57
Equal Rights Amendment (ERA), 84
Ethnic cleansing, 6
Ethnic composition, 6–9
Ethnic survival, 55–58
European Immigrants, 24–26
Expectations, 11, 13, 24, 45, 67

Family, 17, 34, 38, 43
Feinstein, Dianne, 89
Feminists of color, 88
Ferraro, Geraldine, 84
Filipinos, 33
Fitzwater, Marlin, 77
Flathead Lake resort, 41
Food, 13
Football, 60
Franks, Gary, 48
Fuentes, Carlos, 16–17

Gambling, 41
Gantt, Harvey, 48
Ghetto life, 43, 44–45, 68, 75
Ginzburg, Irina, 24
Goode, Wilson, 47–48
Grosz, Gabe, 56
Guidance counselors, 67
Gulf War, 83

Haitians, 23
Haq, Syed Faz, 30
Hate crimes, 63, 72

Hate groups, 73–74
Hayashi, Dennis, 64
Hill, Anita, 84, 86–87
Hispanic Americans, 6, 8, 14–19
Hmong, 36–37
Homer, John, 40
"Hyphenated-Americans," 57

Illegal Aliens, 14, 19, 26
Immigrant, The, 12
Immigrants
    exploitation of, 17
    success rate of, 13
Immigration, 10–13
Immigration Reform Law of 1986, 10
Income, 8, 21, 22–23, 27–28, 43, 46, 82
Indian art and tourism, 41
Indochinese women, 28
Institute for the Recruitment of Teachers, 68
Intermarriage, 32, 41, 55–57
International Ladies Garment Workers Union (ILGWU), 29
Interrace, 56
Irish immigrants, 9, 26
Issues
    education, 11–13, 65–69
    English language, 11, 17, 28, 29, 31
    ethnic identification, 57
    income gap, 82, 92
    political vs. economic refugees, 23
    racism in sports, 59
    skilled vs. unskilled jobs, 29
    Spanish-speaking population, 16

Jackson, Jesse, 15, 18, 51–54, 71, 78
Jamaica, 20
"Japan-bashing," 64
Japanese Americans, 28
Jemison, Mae Carol, 50
Jews, 24
Jobs, 29, 31, 33, 35, 41, 78–80
Johnson, James, 78
Justice, 61–64

Karenga, Maulana Ron, 45
King, Rodney, 75, 76
Kircher, Gwen, 46
Klanwatch, 73–74
Korean Americans, 31, 34, 76–77
Kozol, Jonathon, 65
Ku Klux Klan, 48, 72–73
Kwanzaa, 45
Kwanzaa: An African American Celebration of Culture and Cooking (Copage), 45

Laguna Industries, 41
Language problems, 34, 36, 64, 65
Laotians, 36
Lee, Spike, 44
Lewis, John, 91
Life expectancy, 43–44

Ligon, Alfred, 80
Linares, Guillermo, 16
"Little Saigon," 36
LL Cool J, 45
Los Angeles riots (1992), 75–80
Los Angeles Times, 78

McNair, Ronald, 50
Malcolm, Ellen R., 90
Mandela, Nelson, 49
Mayors, minority, 15, 47–48, 49
Media, 74, 84, 86
Metzger, Tom, 73
Mexican immigrants, 10
Mien, 36
Mikulski, Barbara, 85, 87
Miles, Olivia, 79–80
Mills, Candice, 56
Morrison, Toni, 44
Moscow on the Hudson, 12
Movies, 12, 32, 44
"Mud people," 73
Multicultural curriculum, 69
Multiracial Americans, 56
Murder cases, 62
Murray, Patty, 89, 90
Murray, Reverend Cecil, 76
Music, 45

National Aeronautics and Space
    Administration (NASA), 50
National Guard, 77
National Organization for Women
    (NOW), 83
Native Americans, 6, 39–42
    Zuni, 42
Navajo Reservation and Trust, 40
Neo-Nazi societies, 73–74
New York City, 10–13, 16
New York *Daily News*, 11
New York Times, 93
Ngan, Lang, 11–12

Operation Breadbasket, 51
Order of Aryan Nations, 73

Pakistan Day Festival, 30
Pakistani Americans, 30, 38
Pang, Yun, 31–32
Parenti, Michael, 74
Patu, Betty, 68
Pelotte, Donald E., 39
People United to Serve Humanity
    (PUSH), 52
Pezzolo, Francesco, 59
Planned Parenthood, 86
Police, 62–63, 75
Political power, 7, 15, 46–47, 83

Population, 6–10
Population diversity, 6–9, 10
Poverty, 8, 32, 42, 44, 82
Powwows, 40
Presidential cabinet, 93
Progress, 92–93
Protest marches, 53, 70–71

Quayle, Dan, 77
Quayle, Marilyn, 81

Racial conflict, 70–74
Racism, 59, 61, 64, 72–74
Rainbow Coalition, 52–53
Rap, 45
Receiving stations, 35
Recession, 8, 19, 26, 28, 82
Reed, Adolph, 77
Refugees, 10, 12, 22–23, 37
Reservations, 40, 41, 46
Resurrection City, 52
Rethinking Columbus (Bigelow), 69
Riots, 16, 75–80
Rivera, Dennis, 18
Robinson, Frank, 59, 60
Russian immigrants, 24–26

St. Tikon's Russian Orthodox monastery,
    57
Sam, Chanthou, 37
Sanger, Margaret, 86
Sassen, Saskia, 21
Savage Inequalities (Kozol), 65
Schlafly, Phyllis, 83, 84
School system, 64, 65–69, 92
Schroeder, Pat, 84, 85
Self-employment, 13, 17, 32, 41, 57, 80
Seraw, Mulugeta, 73, 74
Sexism, 88
Sexual Harassment, 86–87
*She Went to War: The Rhonda Cornum
    Story*, 83
Shell, Art, 60
Siv, Sinchan, 28
Skinheads, 73, 74
Smith, Anna Deavere, 70
Smith, Claire, 59
South Pacific Drop-Out Prevention
    Program, 68
Space program, 50
"Special education" classes, 67
Sports, 59–60
Stallings, Steven, 41
Statistics
    arrests, 61–62
    Black mayors, 47–48
    damages of Los Angeles riots, 77
    ethnic population rate, 6–8

hate groups, 73–74
income rate, 8, 22–23
intermarriage, 32, 41, 57
minorities as sports executives, 59–60
minorities in police departments, 62
multicultural states, 7–8
New York City immigrant population,
    10–11
poverty rate, 8, 42
school enrollment, 65–66
self-employment rate, 13
substance abuse, 61
women in politics, 89
women working, 81
Strangers from a Different Shore (Takaki),
    29
Stuart, Michael, 62
Substance abuse, 61
Suburbs, 28, 29, 44

Takaki, Ronald, 29, 32, 37, 64
Teachers, 68
Test scores, 66
Textbooks, 69
Third and fourth generation Americans,
    28, 58
Thomas, Clarence, 84, 87
Thornton, Russell, 39
Tor, Sathaya, 37

Unemployment, 34, 41, 43, 78–79
Unions, 17, 18, 64
United Farm Workers of America
    (UFWA), 17, 64
United Klans of America (UKA), 74
United States Civil Rights Commission,
    63

Valencia, Antonio, 18–19
Vietnamese Americans, 32, 35–36
Vincent, Fay, 60
Voter registration, 30, 53–54
Voting rights laws, 47, 90

Wall Street Journal, 31
Washington, Harold, 47
Waters, Maxine, 78
Wattleton, Faye, 86
West, Cornel, 79
West Indian festival, 71
West Indies, 20–23
West Side Story, 12
White, Bill, 60
White Anglo-Saxon Protestants
    (WASPS), 55
White Aryan Resistance, 73, 74
White supremacy, 72–74
Women, 81–88, 89–91